Mount Kailash The White Mirror
Ngari, Tibet

Nyima Samkar

Library of Tibetan Works & Archives

Subject   : Mount Kailash The White Mirror, Ngari Tibet
Author   : Nyima Samkar

ISBN: 978-93-87023-85-7

Design and layout : Kunsang Choedon
Cover design   : Sonam Dawa
Software used   : Adobe Indesign CS4
Typeset in   : Adobe Garamond Pro, 12pt

Published by Library of Tibetan Works and Archives, Dharamshala, India.
Printed at VEE ENN Print-O-Pac, New Delhi-110020

This book is dedicated to

His Holiness the 14th Dalai Lama

Tenzin Gyatso of Tibet

Contents

Contents

Publisher's Note

❖

This book is a travelogue of Mount Kailash covering almost all the historical and spiritual places of the area in. On reading it, I felt that if Gedun Chophel, the most famous Tibetan scholar of the twentieth century, had added a chapter on visiting Mount Kailash visit to his Grain of Gold (*gTam rgyud gser gyi thang ma*), it would resemble this very book: *Mount Kailash : The White Mirror, Ngari, Tibet.*

This region is the origin of many Asian rivers that eventually reach the Indian Ocean. Mount Kailash and Manasarovara are sacred to all the Asian religions _ Bon, Hinduism, Jainism and Buddhism. Particularly it is the site of great spiritual miracles performed by Kagyupa masters such as Milarepa, including the battle between Milarepa and Naro Bonchung, which is recounted in this book.

The author is a man of simple living and high thinking. He is very intelligent, and has a very good memory and imagination. His close observation of the world is seen clearly through these descriptions if we read between the lines as well. His dream is to visit his homeland, Ruchang, Ngari and let the coming generations understand that the importance and happiness that is gained in one's homeland cannot be imagined elsewhere. Alas, today it is under the occupation of Communist China!

Ngari is a sanctuary of birds and wild animals like antelope, and is free from all kind of pollution. Today we can imagine this is a heaven on earth. Not only has it been mentioned in works of literature, but people today truly understand it and wish to visit Mount Kailash at least once in their lifetime.

The author asked the Library to publish the book, and we happily accepted the request in consulatation with our kind director Geshe Lhakdor la. This book is being published as a part of the publications for the Library Golden Jubilee.

Happy Reading!
Sangye T Naga

Preface

❖

In the good old days I, along with my late parents and relatives, had made a few holy trips around Manasarovara Mount Kailash and Lake Manasarovara. Due to my tender age, I just enjoyed the trip along with them. I did not pay much attention to the holiness or sacredness of those self-evolved statues, footprints and holy sites. I could not then treasure these in my mind. Yet due to my strong memory power and previous merits, many of those places are still fresh in my mind. I have now been living in exile for more than half of a century and far away from them. I have kept my thoughts lingering around the sacred mountain; it has helped me recollect now more about the Sacred Mountain and the Lake.

In 1958, a year before I left Tibet, that I was fortunate enough to pay my last visit to the holy places with my sister, who still remains in Tibet. I had been lucky enough to visit and circumambulate this holy mountain along with my late uncle Choying, who expired in 1963. He was a great tantric practitioner and had circumambulated Mount Kailash thirteen times. Once he even circumambulated Mount Kailash by prostrations Sacred Mountain and the Lake Mount Kailash.

I really do not know what he had in his mind at that time. He showed and explained to me in detail all the places around Mount Kailash and Manasarovara Lake. Again I could not keep them all in my memory, being tender in age and illiterate at that time. I can never revisit the holy place, yet many of the holy areas remain still fresh in my mind. I tried to keep my memory alive and updated with information by telling tales to strangers and trying to acquire more information from our elders.

Time has kept on running and years have rolled by since then. As I grow older, my love for spending time circumambulating and observing all holy places has grown still stronger. This sacred mountain haunts me time and again. And now I am more than a bit literate.

Alas! Tibet, my motherland (normally, we Tibetans call our country the fatherland) is occupied and dominated by the Chinese and they are ruling in their own ways and with their whims and fancies, altering history to suit their stance and making propaganda in order to humiliate Tibet and Tibetans inside and outside the country.

Due to this political situation in Tibet, my passion to revisit Mount Kailash and Manasarovara Lake has remained just a dream. But to quench my thirst for a trip to the Sacred Mountain and the Lake. I have tried my best to circumambulate Mount Kailash and Manasarovara Lake and their surrounding holy places by glimpsing them through books. While visiting the holy sites through the books, I have also learned many new things. I am more and more anxious now to make a trip to Mount Kailash. My children and the children of their generation need valid and solid information about Mount Kailash and Manasarovara Lake. I have a special responsibility to leave behind an authentic information book for the coming generations in case I breathe my last in exile. I am second generation educated who has been to Mount Kailash and Manasarovara Lake when Tibet was free, sovereign and independent, and I happen to know all about it. Writing this monograph also serves in a way my desire for this sacred mountain. I have tried my best to give detailed information of the holy sites and their history, based on reliable books written by great scholars and renowned writers of modern period, who had lived and circumambulated Mount Kailash and Manasarovara Lake; and I spent a number of years with western travelers who visited this mountain in recent times.

Great efforts have also been made to write this book with sincere and careful reference to precious religious books about Mount Kailash and Manasarovara Lake written by high lamas of the Kagyu sect and recently published travel guide books written by well-known writers and explorers.

I have written in this book about caves, monasteries, footprints, idols and various holy places situated at Mount Kailash. I have endeavored to make a detailed description of each and every place that trekkers, researchers and the holy pilgrims should visit during their pilgrimage to the sacred land and readers will note down the places with auspicious associations and also observe palpable piety for those followers who have circumambulated and will circumambulate later on.

The deities, holy places and abodes mentioned in this book are recognized as holy as experienced and visualized by great lamas. By and large, all our great saints and lamas such as Guru Rinpoche, Lopon Sangay Sangwa, Jowo Je Palden Atisha, Dharma Pala, Jetsun Milarepa, Dogon Tsangpa Gyare, Gyawa Gotsang Gonpo Dorje, Nyonlha Nangpa, Dutop Taktse and others have blessed and sanctified the holy places with sincere worship and profound veneration.

There is some vital information for modern trekkers who wish to make a great adventure in their own lifetime to enjoy the highland landscapes and avail themselves of an opportunity to peep inside the fascinating world of esteemed spiritualism.

My narration here is objective. It is neither decorating with lofty feathers nor casting slander and abuse, nor exaggerating the narration with unnecessary criticisms.

There have been quite a number of persons who have come forward to lend their cooperation while writing this book. Space does not allow me to write all the names of those people in detail. I would, however like to express my sincere and deep gratitude to Mr Lobsang Acharya, Director, Research and Analysis Wing (Department) (CTA); Mr Ngawang Namgyal, Additional Secretary of Assembly of People's Deputies (CTA), and the late Mr. Harihar Raj Joshi, former Executive President of The Nepal Studies: Past and Present, for their kind cooperation while I was writing this book. My sincere thanks to Mr Tsering Chophel, founding President of Ngari Chithun Association, who encouraged me to write this book, and am equally happy to bring it out after living 55 years in exile on the auspiciuous 80th Birth Day celebration of our beloved Spiritual and temporal leader of Tibet, His Holiness the Fourteenth Dalai Lama. Due to my financial constraints, I could not bring out many photos. I express my sincere thanks to Mr. Thupten Samphel, General Secretary of DIIR, CTA, Dharamsala for writing an introduction to this book.

Gurub Gongyuetsang Nyima Samkar

Introduction

❖

Ngari, that vast of grassland in western Tibet, is blessed by Mount Kailash and Lake Manasarovara. Tibetans call the Mountain, *Gang Rinpoche* or the Precious Mount. Ngari along with the mountain and the lake have inspired myths and legends of an early paradise, beyul, a hidden land, of Shambala and Shangri-la, the place of eternal youth. Ngari historically was the centre of Zhangzung, the Bon Kingdom, that took within its ambit vast stretches of the Tibetan upland and

Ladakh in India, neighboring Afghanistan and present - day Tajikistan. Its location allowed it to receive fresh ideas and perspective from non-Tibetans to lay the foundation of the earliest culture and traditions of the Tibetan people.

For the Tibetan people, Ngari holds special place because it is where Mount Kailash and Lake Manasarovara are located, the abode of Dechog and his consort, Dorje Phagmo. The Hindus consider Kailash to be the Mount Meru, the core of the universe and the navel of the earth. Charles Allen, the author of *a Mountain in Tibet*, says this myth, "spread with only minor variations as far afield as Japan and Java; the archetypal image of a mountain at the hub of the world from which four mighty rivers take their sources".

Besides Tibetan Buddhists and Bonpos and Hindus, Mount Kailash and Lake Manasarovara are also held sacred by the Jains. Four great religions look to hold Ngari sacred because of Mount Kailash and Lake Manasarovara. It is rare in any place in the world for one place to be object of reverence of four spiritual traditions.

Gurub Gongyuetsang Nyima Samkar's book on his native holy places of Ngari, Kailash and Manasarovara is a work of love and devotion. It is a welcome addition to the growing and rich literature on Ngari, Mount Kailash and Lake Manasarovara. Gurub Gungyuetsang Nyima Samkar makes his book serve as both a hymn and a guide to devotees who may wish to go on a pilgrimage to this holiest of sites in his native Ngari. The author explains the spiritual significance of Mount Kailash and Tso Mapham, the great Tibetan spiritual master, who meditated before the mountain and on the shores of the lake. He gives a brief history of the region and explores the great monasteries of the region and their histories. Both Tibetan and non-Tibetans will appreciate his work on one of the most sacred sites on the planet.

Thupten Samphel
General Secretary
Department of Information and International Relations,
Central Tibetan Administration, Dharamsala,
Himachal Pradesh.

The Mount Kailash

❖

The Mount Kailash, the abode of eternal snow, befittingly known as the king of mountains, animated by Divinity as its soul and internal spirit (or in other words, Divinity Incarnate). It lies in the western Tibet, Ngari, which is popularly called the "Roof of the World", very close to the sun, the moon and the stars.

Expanding across the wide land from the eastern to the western sea, it stands as if it was identical to or resembling to oneself the measuring rod of earth. At the direction of King Prithu, this very mountain was used as a calf by all other mountains, while the Mount Kailash stood as an expert milker of cows and milched the Mother Earth (as if from a cow) the milk of shining gem and medicinal herbs of wonderful virtues and supreme efficacy in order to adorn the Himalaya.

Ngari, in the western part of Tibet, is a place of mysterious and sacred mountains and lakes and of historical sites. It is situated at a driving distance of 1,338 kilometers via western route and 2,021 kilometers via the northern route from Lhasa, the capital of Tibet. This wonderful land of Tibet is said to be, "The Third Pole on the Earth". This holy mountain is associated with our tantric meditational deity or ཡི་དམ་ called Samvara, Eternal Bliss (བདེ་མཆོག), and consort Vajravārāhī (ཕྱག་རྡོ་རྗེ་འཕགས་མོ།). Dechog (བདེ་མཆོག) or Samvara is an awe-inspiring deity, full of fierce energy. Depictions represent him as having four faces in colors of red, blue, green and white, and each having three eyes. He wears a crown of human skulls and has a tiger skin draped around his waist. His body is blue with his twelve arms each holding a symbolic object like a vajra (thunderbolt), elephant skin, skull cup, bell, dagger and so forth. He tramples two prostrate figures under his powerful feet, and carries a curved knife and skull cup. He holds a Damaru (hand drum) in his one hand and Khatanga (trident) in the other.

His consort also called Dorje Phagmo, with whom he is united in a glory of flame, manifests herself in a naked body which is red in color. In Tibetan paintings and idols, the Shakti or the consort Vajravārāhī is shown clinging on to him in inextricable embrace, interlocked in sexual union. She is associated with a small snow-peak called Tijung, a small pyramidal peak which lies adjacent to the Kailash peak on its western side. Dechog is also associated with two other Tibetan mountains besides Mount Kailash. They are Lapchi in Nyanang in Tibet near Nepal and Tsari, approximately 200 miles east of Lhasa. Tsari is very near to the Indo-Tibet border with Arunachal Pradesh. The Buddhist regard them as mountaingods and as such this tantric meditational or tutelary deity is represented in many sacred thangka paintings.

This mountain is naturally thought to be the home and playground of the highest of the gods, a kind of Tibetan Olympus. It is practically associated with the Buddha along with Arhats or Foe Destroyers (དགྲ་བཅོམ་པ་) and indeed his palace and thrones are located on the summit.Around Mount Kailash, there are more deities sitting in 990 rows with 500 in each. Beside these, Lord Buddha and his five hundred bodhisattvas are said to be residing on the peak of Mount Kailash. As well as these deities, but there are also abodes of several other deities around Mount Kailash. We, ordinary people with ordinary eyes, cannot see them. All these deities can be seen only by the pious few. On important days, the sounds of bells, cymbals and other religious musical instruments are heard on the top of Mount Kailash. As one of the most sacred, prestigious, mysterious mountains of Tibet, Mount Kailash also represents Avalokiteshvara, the Buddha of Compassion. Mount Kailash is the centre of faith and this picturesque Mount Kailash stands like a crystal pagoda in the heart of Ngari of Tibet. Out of reverence, Kailash has been addressed as *Gang Rinpoche* (གངས་ རིན་པོ་ཆེ་) Snow Jewel Mountain, and *Gang Tise* meaning mountain of Ice, cool and soothing.

Being the pure realm of Avalokiteshvara, the Buddha of Compassion, Mount Kailash is the centre of pilgrimage for Buddhists that quest for peace and salvation from suffering and freedom from misery for all beings. At the centre of the complex stands a pyramid of rock and snow, towering above the surrounding mountains, as the Tibetans say 'like the handle of the mill stone'. Deep clefts on either side isolate it from the rest of the range, which makes it especially suitable for devotional acts of circumambulation, known as *parikrama*, practiced by Buddhists and followers of other religions.

In modern times, the most important Buddhist association seems to be with Milarepa, the great poetic guru, who lived at this mountain in the late eleventh century and early twelfth century CE during the glorious period of the Guge Kingdom. This great yogic practitioner and poet was a disciple of Marpa, the Great Translator of the Kagyu school of Tibetan Buddhism. Most Tibetan thangka or other paintings of this great yogi show him with his right hand cupped to his ear. His body is a strange greenish or greyish color as a result of his having lived exclusively on nettles. Milarepa was synonymous with Mount Kailash, because he was involved in a direct struggle for the possession of Mount Kailash with Naro Bonchung, the highest priest of the Bon faith of that time.

Ngari is situated at the meeting point of the Himalaya where the Mount Kailash and Karakoram ranges are at an approximate altitude of 4500 meters above sea level. The exact height of Mount Kailash measured at 6714 meters above the sea level in the heart of Ngari, and the height of its surrounding area is about 4700 meters above sea level. This land has aptly been called the pinnacle of the world.

This holy mountain is not only a center for Buddhist practitioners, but also a sacred place for Hindus, Jains and Bon followers. Hindus regard Mount Kailash as the sacred abode of Lord Shiva and his consort goddess Parvati. In the Hindu religion, Lord Shiva is the god of mighty mountains, a great lord of yogic wanderers and mystics, and is often portrayed seated in a lotus position on a tigerskin, ash smeared and clad only in a deerskin. Goddess Parvati Devi is Lhamo Uma in her peaceful form whereas in her fierce form she is popularly known as Durga or Kalimata (དཔལ་ལྡན་ལྷ་མོ།). Her elevation represents a significant development in the Hindu religion; worship of the female principle has always been present in the religions of the Indian sub-continent.

Only a few historians believe that Aryans came to India from Tibet. The majority of historians say that they came to India from Central Asia. When the Aryans came to India, they established Meru, the mountain of blazing appearance, as the central core of the universe and the navel of the earth. The Aryans hold that Mount Meru is situated beyond and to the north of the bright gold dwellings. Here, the sun, moon and other heavenly planets take their orbit around this mountain. The Pole Star stands directly above its summit. Here, we will find palaces and thrones of the gods and celestial beings, headed by Brahma the Creator, with lesser deities and saints inhabiting a less exalted plain tower down the mountain. Naturally, this mountain is regarded as the home and playground of the highest of the Gods, a kind of Hindu Olympus. As for its other high qualities like shape, colour and composition, accounts vary. This mountain may be gold, luminous, or multi in red, white, yellow and dark. It may be shaped like an inverted cone, or a saucer, or a parallelepiped. It may be quadrangular, octangular, hundred angles or even thousand angled. Leading up to Mount Meru was the pathway of the stars, land of fragrant trees and flowers, where the souls of the dead awaited rebirth. Tibetans had the same viewpoint. We believed in ancient time that this mountain was only mythical and that we ordinary people even cannot even see the mountain. The details of Tibetan viewpoints will be given in a later chapter.

The Puranas have mentioned that Mount Meru is stands at the centre of a complex multi-dimensional system embracing both the material and spiritual dimensions. The reputed height of Mount Meru is mind-boggling. A figure of 84,000 yojanas is often cited. It is difficult to give an accurate equivalent to a yojana, estimates by scholars and translators vary from as little as a league to as much as 14 kilometers. Probably, the best way to view the 84,000 yojanas is as a figurative expression denoting sheer vastness of the altitude, as John Snelling, in the "*The Sacred Mountain, [published 1991 by East-West Publications (U.K.) Ltd]*" states,

It was during an early 1974 that I got a rare opportunity to go along with a group of Belgium Professors with Heinrich Harrer visit Alaknanda and its surrounding areas. During that time, I could luckily visit Badrinath Temple and its surrounding areas too. We were briefed by an army colonel (forgot his name) who was stationed at Badrinath, that once Lord Shiva was living at Badrinath, a perfect place situated like a lap of heaven rich in the floras and surrounded by high majestic mountains. A land of peace and tranquility and one could really realize Sunyuta. Later on, Vishnu came to this place and he controlled the area and made his permanent abode there. So ultimately, Shiva had to leave this place. Some time before his departure, Shiva was residing in the opposite side of the present Badrinath temple on the riverbank. He felt sad to leave this wonderful place in the lap of heaven, and his eyes moistened and his heart beat fast and two powerful drops of tears rolled down from his eyes. There appeared a huge rock with two big eyes and two turquoise color ponds appeared at the site. As tears rolling down from the eyes never meet, so these two ponds never meet. Shiva left for the Mount Kailash and he found it as the best place for his permanent residence. Further, Col. Sahib told us that later on

Shiva's parents tried to leave Badrinath and go to the Mount Kailash to live along with Lord Shiva. On their way, they were old and they rested beside the rock and prayed for their son Shiva. Both of them died on the spot, and there appeared two marble snake-shaped prints on the rock. This rock with two snake prints is located between Badrinath and Mana village.

We made our camp near this site and stayed there for ten days. It was early spring and a few Hindu pilgrims were arriving at the Holy Temple of Badrinath and these pilgrims never missed to visit the rock with two snake prints. It is said that there were two foot prints left on his way to Kailash before we cross the Mana Pass. The Mana pass is gateway to Guge kingdom. Tsarang is situated 75 Kilometers away from the Mana Pass. As it was too early in the year and due to the heavy snowfalls during previous winter, we could not see the footprint during our visit to Mana side. The Badrinath temple is situated on the steep river bank of the Gangotri River. A black stone idol occupied the inner sanctum and has its own mythology. The statue is in form and posture of a Buddhist Bodhisattva. The Buddhists claim that this statue and temple were established during the golden period of Ashoka in the third century BC. But after the fall of Ashoka's empire, Buddhism declined in India a few centuries later with the spread of Hinduism. The great Hindu teachers started their conversion and they denied the existence of all the Buddhist shrines on this particular place. They even claimed that there existed Hindu shrines even earlier than the Vedic periods. All the more, I never took it seriously about the legend of area, as I never thought that one day I would have to write something about the Kailash and its related stories.

People consider the renowned Mount Sumeru mentioned in the Buddhist texts as simply a mythical or imaginary place. This is, however, not true. From an academic point of view, Mount Kailash has been a sacred mountain since the dawn of human history. This Mount Kailash is the real Mount Sumeru. Lord Buddha prophesied in one of his teachings at Bodhgaya about

Mount Kailash. In the Tripitaka (Abhidharma shastra), Lord Buddha said that upon heading northward through Central India, and crossing nine snow-mountains, one would arrive at a huge snow mountain, and that is Mount Kailash. Whatever earlier classical traditional belief may have maintained, now in the modern day, numerous scholars and writers agree that Mount Kailash and Mount Meru were regarded as the one and the same mountain.

Prior to the advent of Buddhism, this mountain was a venerated place of the Bonpos. But its importance in more recent times was certainly because of the influence of the Kagyu School. This mountain has been associated with the great poet and tantric yogi, who made his own teacher's teachings to a great extent succeed to provide leadership of the Tibetan religious school of Kagyud in Buddhist religion, after the death of his own teacher, Marpa, the great translator, the founder of the school.

The land of Ngari is the centre of pilgrimage. According to a Tibetan legend, the Kunlun mountain range situated on the northern side of Ngari is the abode of immortals. The Kunlun lies 8610 metres above the level of the even bosom of the sea. In the same direction also lies five-peaked Nanda Devi at 8120 metres. This mountain is believed to be the reincarnation of Goddess Parvati with her four daughters, venerated by Tibetans as well as Hindus.

Mount Kailash is situated in the heart of the Zhangzhung kingdom and was held by Bonpos till the time of Milarepa. The founder of the Bon religion is said to have peeped from heaven and seen the Mount Kailash region as a perfect and suitable place to be its stronghold. The Bon text recount that the nine-storey swastika mountain at the heart of their religion had to be moved to its present site from north - eastern Tibet, which may well refer to the migration of Mongolian people across Tibet that took place about two thousand years earlier (Allen 1990).

Mount Kailash was the centre of the Bon faith with the appearance of Tonpa Shenrab (the founder of Bon) at that place. The Bon religion was mainly related with mountains gods and lake deities. The Bonpos held held in special awe those places with an association with certain ancestral gods, bestowing upon them the status of the soul of a region. Mount Kailash was the soul mountain of the Zhangzhung kingdom.

This mountain towered above the swarga (Heaven or Dewachen Zhingkham) like a parasol with eight ribs and above the earth like an eight petal with swastikas. It was the navel of the world, the seat of goddess of Sky-walkers (མཁའ་འགྲོ་) and dwelling of 360 arhats. The Bon scriptures also describes that it was imagined as a great chorten (stupa) of crystal rocks, and as a palace where several families of the mountain god resided. Mount Kailash has four directions with four gates, one at each cardinal point guarded respectively by the tiger (སྟག), the tortoise (རུས་སྦལ་), the garuda (བྱ་ཁྱུང་།) and the dragon (འབྲུག).

This mountain has been the seat of the followers of the Bon religion, and it was the capital of Zhangzhung during the period of Tonpa Shenrab, the founder of the Bon religion. This is the place where the founder of the religion descended from the heaven to the earth. Bon is the earliest religion of the region; it flourished before bloom before the advent of Buddhism in Tibet.

According to Dzamling Ganggyal Tisei Karchag ('Dzam gling Gangs rgyal Tisei dkar chags), importance was bestowed upon the Gang Tise region during the reign of the first Zhangzhung king. Scripture states,

ཞང་ཞུང་ཡུལ་གྱི་དབུས་གནས་ཀྱི་བདག་མ་སྟོང་ལྡན་ལྷ་བུའི་དབུས་དཀྱིལ།

གངས་རི་ཆེན་པོའི་མཐུན་རྫང་།

རི་སྤོས་རི་དད་ལྡན་ཀྱི་ར་བ།

མཚོ་མུ་ལེ་ཁྱུང་ཀྱི་འགྲམ་དུ་བབས་ཅིང་།

འགྲོ་བ་ཀུན་ཀྱི་ལྷ་སྐལ་དུ་བབས་ཅིང་བྱིན་ཀྱིས་རླབས་པ་དང་།

ཁྱད་པར་སྐྱོ་འཛམ་བུ་གླིང་གི་དབུས།

གངས་རི་ཆེན་པོའི་མདུན་ཞོལ་དུ།

གསས་ཁང་ནོར་བུ་སྤུངས་རྩིགས་བཞེངས་པ་ལ་སོགས་བྱིན་གྱིས་

རླབས་ཚུལ་མང་དུ་ཡོད་པའོ།།

zhang zhung yul gyi dbus gser gyi pad ma stong ldan lta bui
    dbus dkyil,
Gangs ri chen poi mdun drung, Ri spos ri ngad ldan gyi
    rtsa ba,
mtsho mule khyud kyi dram du babs cing,
'Dro ba kun gyi lha skal du babs cing byin gyis rlabs pa dang,
Khyad par lho 'dzam bu gling gi dbus,
    Gangs ri chenpoi mdun zhol du,
gSas khang nor bu spungs rtsigs bzhengs pa la sogs byin gyis
    rlabs tshul mang du yod pa'o.

In the centre of Zhangzhung country, which is like a thousand petalled golden lotus, there is Gang Rinpoche. In front of it, at the base of Mount Po-ri Ngad dan (sPos-ri Ngad-ldan, Fragrant Incense Mountain), there is the lake Mule khyud and on its shore, the Tonpa (Lord) appeared. During the auspicious days in the world at that time, Triwer Larje Gulang (Khri Wer La rJe Gu lang), the holder of the crown of the horns of bird, lived at the Tise. When the Great Lord (sTonpa) appeared at Tise, King Khri Wer La rJe and his subjects, Lha, kLu and others residing at the Tise were blessed with the divine gifts of Lord Tonpa Shenrab, in particular, the Se Khang Norbu Pungtsig (gSas Khang Norbu sPungs rtsigs) established in front of the great snow mountain (Gang Tise). In the middle of the south continent, they received the manifold blessings and the prime benefaction of the founder of the Bon religion.

J.V. Bellezza (1997) aptly said in his book, "This account helps to explain us why the Gang Rinpoche is the residence of the first Zhangzhung king held in such high esteem by the

Bonpos and why it is thought to have been the religious hub of Zhangzhung". Bon scripture has this important reference:

དེ་ཚེ་སླ་སྐུ་མི་སོ་གནས་ཀུན་འདུས་ཏེ།
དེའི་ནང་ཁྱབ་པར་ཞང་ཞུང་སྲིད་པའི་རྒྱལ་པོ།
ཁྲི་ཕྱེར་གསེར་གྱི་བྱུ་རུ་ཅན་ཞེས་པ་དེས།
གསེར་སོ་གནས་རིན་ཆེན་སླ་ཚོགས་མཆོད་པ་ཕུལ།
གུས་པའི་ཆུལ་གྱིས་ཞུས་ཅིང་གསོལ་བ་བཏབ།
སྟེ་ར་གཡུང་དྲུང་བསྟན་པ་དར་བ་དང་།
སྲོས་སུ་བདག་གཞན་ཚོགས་རྟགས་སྟིབ་སྲུངས་པའི།
གཡུང་དྲུང་གསང་བའི་བོན་སྒྲིད་གནང་པར་ཞུས།
སྲོན་པས་ཞལ་ནས་ཁྲི་རྗེ་ལྱུང་བསྟན་པའི།
བོན་སྒྲིད་མདོ་སྟེ་སུམ་ཅུ་རྟགས་པར་གསུངས།

With the advent of Kagyu Tibetan tradition, especially the Drigungpas, Mount Kailash became very famous for Buddhists. It became the seat of Kagyupa practitioners and other Tibetan Buddhist sects, and a centre of faith and inspiration for all Tibetans. The holy saints who had been to Mount Kailash unanimously authenticated its sacredness and its power to do away with ignorance and bestow blessing. Practically, the Bonpos were wiped out from the Mount Kailash and Manasarovara; their retreat caves were claimed by Kagyupa retreatants and yogis, and their small shrine castles were replaced by various Buddhist monasteries.

Mount Kailash is not only the embodiment of power, knowledge, beauty, coolness, water and jewels, but also the source of civilization of Ngari. In ancient times, the great sages spent time at this mountain meditating and on retreat. Aswaghosh (སློབ་དཔོན་རྟ་དབྱངས།), great Hindu scholar born in (80--150 CE) spent 12 years meditating on Lord Shiva and his consort Parvati while staying at the Lake Kapali at the back of Mount Kailash. Eventually, he achieved a spiritual visualisation through his long meditation and received a shakti, a supernatural power. Lord Shiva and his consort Parvati appeared in front of him and asked spiritual power he wished to have bestowed on him. With great joy, he demanded that he should be given the spiritual power that no human being could defeat him in debate on religious matters. They willingly blessed him in defense of the religion. This powerful Hindu scholar then often went to Nalanda to have great religious debates with the Buddhist scholars and other. Due to the super power bestowed upon by Shiva, he won a number of debates with the Buddhist monks at Nalanda. The Buddhist scholar Asanga, who was not born by a natural birth, was able to at last defeat Aswaghosh. After the defeat, he converted to Buddhism, took the name Acharya Vira, and became one of the greatest Buddhist scholars. He wrote a commentary on the Buddhist scriptural work known as མཚོ་སྒྲེ་དྲུན་པ་ཞེར་གཞག Later on, he was known as Viracharya for his heroic devotion to the cause of Buddhism. The Tibetans addressed him as Lopon Pawo.

Jain believers consider Mount Kailash to be a spiritually peak; the place where the first prophet of their faith purged himself of sins before he began to preach. They also consider Mount to be the pillar of the earth, around which the entire universe revolves, as well as the terrestrial manifestation of Mount Meru.

Charles Allen in his book (2003), *A Mountain in Tibet*, has mentioned that in ancient Chinese records of the western world compiled during the Tang dynasty (618--907 CE), the mountain called Sumeru stands up in the midst of the great sea firmly fixed on a circle of gold around which the sun and moon revolve. Four precious substances make this mountain perfect and it is the abode of the devas (gods). There are seven mountain ranges and seven seas around this mountain.

In the middle of the Shan-pu-chao (the central continent), there is a lake known as Wo-jo-nao-chih, which is to the south of the fragrant mountain and to the north of the great snowy mountains. It measures 800 li around.[1] Its sides are composed of gold, silver, lapis lazuli and crystal. Golden sands lie at the bottom and its waters are clear as a mirror. The wall of Great Earth Bodhisattva transformed him into a Nagaraja (Serpent king) who dwells therein. From his dwelling the cool water extended further and enriched Shan-pu chao.

In geological terms, Mount Kailash has the world's highest deposit of tertiary conglomerate, a vast pile of cemented gravel laid down in the period immediately preceding the arrival of early man and then thrown up above the sky. It has four clearly defined walls that match the points of the compass, and on its southern face a deep gully that runs from the summit, cutting across an equally distinctive rock band of horizontal strata. This is the mark that has earned the Kailash the title of the "Swastika mountain" གཡུང་དྲུང་རི།". It is the southern face, emblazoned with its talisman of spiritual strength, the swastika, that the pilgrim first sees as he ascends out of India. Kailash is on the horizon and, occupying much of the depression in the middle distance, what was formerly a large circular lake with an island at its centre is now two lakes divided by a narrow isthmus of high ground.

Charles Allen writes that this Himalayan holy land had been thoroughly explored by the time the first of the sacred texts known as the "Puranas" came to be written, allowing the basic cosmography of the Mahabharata to be expanded into a more solid and realistic Asian geography. Altogether, there were eighteen Purana texts compiled over a period of thousand years from about 200 BCE to 800 CE. The best known and oldest Purana is the Vishnupurana. It is believed to have been written in the second century BCE. One of its chapters describes how

____

1 Traditional Chinese miles, equivalent to approximately 400 kilometres.

the world is made up of seven continents surrounded by seven oceans. The central island has Meru at its core, bounded by three mountain ranges to the north and three to the south, lying between them "like the pericarp of a lotus". One of the ranges is the Himalayan barrier, interposed between Meru and the Indian sub-continent (Bharat). The world-pillar itself stands eighty four thousand leagues high, with four faces of crystal, ruby, and gold and lapis lazuli. From the heavens or, more precisely, from the nail in the great toe of Vishnu's left foot falls "the stream that washes away all sin".

The Tantra of the Great Liberation found in the Mahaparina tantra (trans. Arthur Avalon (Sir John Woodroffe) described Kailash as appended below,

"The enchanting summit of the Lord of Mountains, resplendent with all its varied jewels, clad with many a tree and many a creeper, melodious with the song of many a bird, scented with the fragrance of all the season's flowers, most beautiful, fanned by soft, cool, and perfumed breezes, shadowed by the still shade of stately trees; where cool groves resound with the sweet-voiced songs of troop of Apsara (heavenly nymphs) and in the forest depths flocks of kokila (cuckoos) maddened with passion sing; where (spring) the Lord of the season with his followers ever abide".

Many revered high lamas who visited this mountain ardently eulogized with true religious spirit their view of its great wonder. They had undergone enormous hardship while trekking to this holy mountain from their hometowns. They came here for circumambulation, meditation and prostration. Some of the ascetics and the hermits resided here for many years, meditating and performing religious activities even without proper food and clothes, because of the lack of food and clothes in the caves especially during the winters when no inhabitants could visit to holy caves.

We have numerous volumes of teachings of our great saints who spent their lives in this mountain. All of them mentioned that Mount Kailash is the most sacred mountain situated in Western Tibet. It is this holy Mount Kailash that Lord Buddha had prophesized at Bodh Gaya as the central place of the world at the time.

According to Buddhist mythology, there are three pilgrimage circuits around Mount Kailash, two circuits are well known to us: the Arhats (དགྲ་བཅོམ་པ།, Foe Destroyers) Sky-Walkers and deities are believed to take the topmost circuit. The accomplished beings take the inner or middle circuit, and the ordinary people take the outer circuit of the mountain.

The distance around Mount Kailash for one circumambulation by the outer circuit is 52 Kilometres. In the old days, the Tibetans normally took one day or 13 to 15 hours to complete one circumambulation. It is advisable to take two days for one circumambulation, so that one can visit and pay due respects to the holy monasteries along the way. One can also have time for sightseeing; for example the panoramic view afforded by the surrounding areas of Mount Kailash while trekking by the outer pilgrimage circuit. On every walk of the ritual route, the way is replete with powerful religious symbolism and auspicious associations. There are many sacred footprints of the Buddha and other religious luminaries, the caves where great yogis lived and pursued their austerities. On the tortuous rocks, virtue could test the minds of pilgrims. There used to be numerous places where the pilgrims should pause and pray and prostrate before the mountain. There also used to be innumerable cairns to which he or she should add a stone of his or her own while passing through these cairns.

A group comprising elderly people, children and infirm persons comfortably completes circumambulating the outer circuit in three days. There are some keen people who prefer to complete one circumambulation around the mountain in a single day. We normally call this flying type of circumambulating the mountain by persons, as "running dog circumambulating". Generally, the flying circumambulation is not admired by religious people, and it is generally considered that pilgrims are less blessed by such kind of circumambulation, if undertaken. Anyone wishing to circumambulate the mountain by performing parikrama, that is by means of prostrating the full length of one's own body, generally takes 15-20 days to complete one circumambulation by the same circuit. Ideally, Tibetans make circumambulate Mount Kailash either thrice or 13 times in their lifetime. In earlier time, some people used to make circumambulation 108 times, and some prostrated as many as they could by the outer circuit. They were preoccupied with various practices of religious activities such as twirling prayer wheels and muttering mantras.

It is believed that a pilgrim can wash away the sins of one lifetime by circumambulating Mount Kailash once. If one walks around the Mount Kailash thirteen times, one will get salvation from the sufferings of the hell realm for 500 future lives. If one circumambulates the Mount Kailash 108 times, one can attain Buddhahood in the next birth. It is believed that if a pilgrim circumambulates the Mount Kailash in a Horse year, one earns more remit for life. Buddha Shakyamuni was born in the Horse year in Lumbini. It is also said that Lord Buddha and his 500 disciples visited Mount Kailash and blessed Mount Kailash in the year of Horse. This mountain can acquire merits "Chakra Jyotisha". (?)

The great saints and individuals used to take the inner pilgrimage twelve times more in comparison to other years. In the year 1027, Pandit Somnath of Kashmir translated the "Kalachakra Jyotisha" དུས་འཁོར་རྩིད་འགྱེལ།" into Tibetan and introduced the Brihaspati cycle of sixty years which we normally term Prabava (རབ་བྱུང་). This cycle of sixty years is divided into five sub-cycles of twelve years each. In each Horse year (རྟ་ལོ་), a big fair is held at on Sershong plain. According to Tibetan scriptures, a ritual circuit made by pilgrims to Holy Kailash and Manasarovara during a horse year is considered as virtuous as thirteen rounds made during other years.

The pilgrimage circuit to circumambulate the holy mountain starts from Dharchen or the Big Flagpole at Sershong Thang (གསེར་གཞོངས་ཐང་།) at the foothill of the Throne of 500 Arhats (Foe Destroyers). For a pilgrim who wishes to take the inner or middle circuit pilgrimage, he or she has to complete 13 rounds of circumambulation or at least, one round of prostration first around the outer circuit.

The inner circuit pilgrimage of Mount Kailash takes pilgrims first to the thirteen-tiered Pagoda, followed by Gyangtak monastery of Drigung Kagyud, then to Sarlung monastery, and back to Dharchen. This place was an important centre of wool trade in the olden days. Even these days, the place has become more important as centre for the Tourism Department due to the flow of western tourists and pilgrims coming from neighboring countries.

There are six monasteries around Mount Kailash:
 * Choeku Monastery in the western foothills of the mountain
 * Driraphuk Monastery in the north
 * Zutrulphuk Monastery on the eastern side
 * Gyangtak Monastery on the western side of Mount Kailash
 * Sarlung Monastery on the western side of Kailash

Tharchen Dolma Lhakhang is built in front of Mount Kailash in the Dharchen area. Dharchen is a trade centre at the base of Mount Kailash. It had a few old houses before 1959. During the trading times, hundreds of tented camps sprung up on the meadows of the vast open plain of Bongtug Zhung. This area belongs to Gangs Sa County of Purang district.

This holy land of Mount Kailash is where not only our highly respected lamas, but also the saints and yoga practitioners among various teachers of Kagyud traditions of Kadriduksum (Kamtsang, Drigung and Drugpa) have visited and blessed. It is very difficult to mention all their names here, as hundreds of highly respected lamas have made their holy trips and sanctified this holy mountain. Some of the renowned and respected teachers and reformers who visited this holy mountain are listed below.

* Atisha played a major role in the second part of the diffusion of Buddhism in Tibet. He visited Mount Kailash in of 1042 CE. When he reached a place called Barkha Tasam, in front of the majestic mountain, Atisha told his disciples that the gods and deities of the holy mountain had rung the bells for their lunch, so it was time for them to prepare the food and make offerings to the gods and deities of Mount Kailash. Atisha and Marpa made their disciples understand Mount Kailash. Marpa's pupil Milarepa and his followers, like Drigung Chonga Lingpa and Guya(Guhaya?) Gangpa, of the new generation of the eleventh century indeed made the Mount Kailash area the scene of great religious activities during the regenerative time of Buddhism from the Guge kingdom.

* In King Gesar's epic named *Gangs-ri'i Shel-rzong (Mountain Glass Fort)*, it is mentioned that once during the reign of mighty king Singchen, his Prince Dalha Tsegya and his courageous minister warriors were proceeding toward Mount Kailash for circumambulation. He saw the mountain as resembling the King of Mountain, Sumeru, covered with silver in the midst of the sky. The top of the mountain was encircled by a five-colored rainbow. King Gesar had a clear vision of the deity Vajradhara, an embodiment of the Truth Body, Avalokiteshvara, the embodiment of the Complete Enjoyment Body, Great Lama Garab Dorjee, the embodiment of the Emanation Body, and other eminent lamas of Kagyudpa tradition all grouped together inside the rainbow.

* The great treasure-revealer Nyima Dakpa said that Gangs Tise is Dechog (bDe-mchog) place, and he received teachings from this great mountain. He also saw Arya Neten Yenlak Jung surrounded by fifteen hundred Arhats (Foe-destroyers) in the middle of Mount Kailash, which appears as the mandala of Deity

Cakrasamvara. At the left side on top of the mountain, there was group of five Sky-Walkers (མཁའ་འགྲོ།) singing and dancing in praise of the great protectors (deities) of Mount Kailash, and making them happy. The great treasure-revealer Nyima Dakpa said that Mount Kailash is a place of Sri Cakrasamvara and it is here that he received the teachings of Dechog.

Arrival of Jetsun Milarepa at Mount Kailash and Manasarovara Lake

Naropa told his great disciple Milarepa to proceed to Mount Kailash, the holy mountain, in order to attain salvation. This mountain was prophesied by Lord Buddha, as perfect and the holiest among the holy mountains of Tibet, and this mountain is the king of mountains of the world. It was necessary for him to meditate there to attain his own enlightenment and for sentient beings in the near future. It was probably Marpa the great translator and Naropa who knew that Milarepa could set up a base for his teachings around Kailash and Manasarovara Lake. Accordingly, Milarepa left for Mount Kailash and reached the holy mountain in 1093.

The local deities of the land cordially welcomed Milarepa, but the Bon figure Naro Bonchung did not like Milarepa's appearance on the Manasarovara shore. Naro Bonchung, an inhabitant of the area, had already heard about Milarepa's fame and reputation and about his mystical magical power. He proudly told Milarepa that as the Bonpos had been in possession of Kailash and Manasarovara Lake for a long time, Milarepa had to change his faith if he wished to spend more time at these holy areas, and conduct his meditational practices at the holy sites. Naro Bonchung was the head of the Bon religion of this period. Bon was flourishing in full blossom, and this mountain was owned by the followers of Bon. Naro Bonchung was the most significant Bon figure of this time and he had spent a number of years at both Kailash and Manasarovara Lake. Despite the difference in belief and practices, both of them possessed tantric magical power. During the beginning of Milarepa's arrival at Kailash, both masters faced problems.

Logically, as two daggers cannot be put in a single sheath, so it is not easy for two great masters of different faiths to live at one place together. One has to gain supremacy over the other, and one has to lose the power and leave the place, which is but a natural phenomenon. Milarepa arrived at Kailash during the supremacy of the Guge kingdom of Ngari and Buddhism was spreading in the area like wildfire; this was a peak time, the later diffusion of Buddha's teaching (sTan pa phyi dhar) (བསྟན་པ་ཕྱི་ དར). It was possible that Milarepa received the royal support to make his teachings stronger than those of Naro Bonchung around Kailash and Manasarovara Lake.

Milarepa, who had already earned a great reputation for his mystical attainments, did not accept the views of Naro Bonchung. He told Naro Bonchung that Lord Buddha had prophesied that one day Kailash and Manasarovara Lake would fall under the sway of the followers of his Dharma. Milarepa further told Naro Bonchung that Mount Kailash had special significance for Milarepa because his great teacher Marpa had asked him to go there. Accordingly, Milarepa went there to meditate not only for his own life but also for all future sentient beings. A series of mystical magic contests was held and Milarepa won the every contest. Naro Bonchung accepted his defeat made a circumambulation of Mount Kailash on an anti clock outer circuit. In one textual script, it is mentioned that numerous mystical magical power contests were held between these two great masters of two different faiths; it is also mentioned that every time Milarepa, won the tantric contest against Naro Bonchung.

The final and the last contests between the two different religious masters were held at the Mount Kailash. The final contest between the two religious masters was held at Mount Kailash itself. It was decided that the first one to climb to the top of Kailash and reach the summit before sunrise on 15th of mChu-zla {etc} would control the holy mountain and, naturally, become the master of Kailash, able to practice and strengthen his teachings around the holy places. The loser would concede defeat in the magic contest, and leave the place. Naro Bonchung, trained in unremitting practices of Bon religious magical power, agreed to compete with Milarepa. In the early morning of the 15th of mChu-zla, Naro Bonchung mounted on his the shaman's magical drum left for the summit of Mount Kailash. Our text says that he was wearing a green cloak and assiduously playing a musical instrument. While flying through the sky on his drum. Naro Bonchung was about to land on the summit of Mount Kailash when the followers of Milarepa caught sight of him

Milarepa was still in his bed deep in meditation, and it was greatly shocking and disturbing to the disciples and followers of Milarepa. However, with a simple gesture, Milarepa stopped the speed of his opponent's upward journey. As day started and the rays of the sun were touching on the mountain, Milarepa snapped his fingers, put on his clothes and was at once soaring up towards the summit. Milarepa appeared on the summit of Mount Kailash just as the first ray of the sunlight arrived at the summit and looked down at Naro Bonchung who was about to conquer the summit of Mount Kailash. Naro Bonchung was shocked and alarmed on seeing Milarepa already on the top. It was said that his drum fell down the southern face of the Kailash, forming a valley and creating avalanches (but in reality, the valley already existing and normally avalanches occurred frequently).

As agreed upon earlier, Naro Bonchung accepted defeat in the spiritual magic contest and left Mount Kailash but first he requested Milarepa that he should be given a place to live near Mount Kailash. Milarepa gave him the Bonri Mountain near Kailash.

From then on, the Bonpos were replaced by Bodhisattvas of such sacred reputation and fame as Dechog Kuyine (bDe-mchog sKuyi gnas) and his consorts Dorje Phagmo (rDo-rje 'Phags-mo). The great tantric yogi Milarepa was historically the first Tibetan yogi directly involved with Mount Kailash. Milarepa himself is often portrayed seated on the holy mountain in our religious texts and paintings. His name is synonymous with Mount Kailash too. The thunderbolt (vajra) tantric school of Buddhism was taught by Milarepa, and its rituals are common among practitioners, as are recitations of the mantra, OM MANI PADME HUM; and this mantra has been inscribed on countless mani stones throughout Tibet, Ladakh, Nepal and Bhutan. All entire Buddhist followers recite this mantra continuously for millions of times. Generally, we call it the Six-Syllable Words (ཡི་གེ་དྲུག), that is OM-MA-NI-PAD-ME-HUM.

Milarepa spent a number of years at Mount Kailash to meditate, sanctifying the mountain, and thus it became a holy place for Buddhists in general and Kagyudpa in particular. Because of Milarepa's meditation practice and blessings of the Mount Kailash, later on many sages of the Kagyudpa tradition spent their lives in meditation there, building monasteries and residing in caves around the mountain. It seems that no other Tibetan Buddhist schools could send as many scholars and tantric practitioners to Mount Kailash as Drigung Kagyud and Drugpa Kagyud did. So in practical terms Holy Kailash belongs to the Drigung in general and Drugpa Kagyud in particular.

For the first time in the history of Ngari, in 1618 CE, His Eminence Lobsang Chokyi Gyaltsen, the Third Panchen Rinpoche of Tashi Lhunpo, paid a holy visit to Ngari Khorsum. During his honorable visit, he took the opportunity to undertake holy pilgrimages to Mount Kailash. It is clearly recounted in his autobiography that he had a vision of Mount Kailash as a palace of Sri Cakrasamvara, as visualized by other and many enlightened beings have visualized Mount Kailash made of precious gem stones measuring a full 500 fathoms (approximately 900 metres) in height. The interior of the mountain is the abode of gods and protector deities of the mountain.

The great saint Drubwang Shabkar Tsokdrug (sDrub-dwang Shabs-dkar Tsogs-drug) says in his autobiography that he used to visit all the holy places in U-Tsang area and went to Mount Kailash. Along the way, he met people who asked him about his destination and the purpose of his journey to which he replied in the form of a verse,

> Of world's Gangkar Tise (Gangs dkar Tisi),
> The wonder Dechog (bDe-mchog) place
> Never had its vision before,
> Today, going to have a look.
>
> The resident of that holy place
> Five hundred wondrous Arhats,
> Never received religious teachings before
> Today, going to receive religious teachings.
>
> In this holy place, assembled
> The wonderful and darling Goddesses.
> Never had friendship together with them,
> Today, going to have friendship.
> In the east of that holy place
> Is the wonder and miraculous cave in which,
> Never had Bodhi meditation before,
> Today, going to practice Bodhi.

Drubwang Shabkar Tsokdrug reached Mount Kailash in 1814. After arriving at the miraculous cave, he prayed and paid great tribute to Mount Kailash, and spent many years there in meditation and gave teachings to the public. In praise of the mountain, he said,

The mountain as prophesied in sutra and tantra
Is the real palace of Rab Byams (*Rab-'byams*) and Gyalwa
    (*rGyal-wa*),
Place of mKha'-'dro (Sky-Walkers) assembly
And is a destination for Gods and saints.

Renowned by the name of Gangkar Tise,
Resembles the shape of mountain to a crystal stupa,
Earlier, in Buddha's prophesy
It has been named Riwo Gangchen (Snow Mountains).

The crystal stupa shaped mountain
Is the abode of deity Dechog,
All boundaries encircled by mountains are
Destination for many Arhats.

Usually, clouded with Buddhas of past, present and future
    like cloud,
mKha'-'dros and protectors gather like servants,
Like turquoise embedded in golden eye,
Every cave has a great yogi (meditator),
Prints of Buddha's foot and deity's bodies etc.

Various wonders can be seen and
Can visualize the miraculous signs and can spring from
    meditation by Mila and Naro Bonchung,
The Two Great Lakes, the Mansarovara and Lanka
    (*Rakshas Tal*).

Embellishes like water bowl and offerings in the front
Many devotees and patrons are in all directions,
Adequate facilities are there for religious practice and
    pleasant
King of birds the golden colour geese, etc,
And various birds melodious chirping makes it happy.

In the miraculous cave of eastern remote area,
Of the special holy place Mount Tise,
I, the pauper, Shabkar Tsokdrug, felt
Good for having opportunity to practice religion.

Kagyud Lamas residing in this place,
May bless (me) for attainment and salvation
May the gods and all protecting deities,
Bless me with extraordinary attainments
May the mkha'-'dros, religious protectors and deities of
    place
Help the pauper to attain Buddhahood.

He stayed for nearly four years until 1818 and gave many teachings to the people of Ngari, and also composed a book of advice for them.

Accordingly, many highly revered spiritual heads of different Tibetan religious orders have visited and paid rich tribute to this mountain. Many holy pilgrims and numerous yogis have spent their lives in various caves and have attained ultimate goal of the "oneness" or Shunyata.

Holy people and the fortunate ones see Mount Kailash as a magnificent, splenddidly majestic, mysterious, high snow-capped mountain with so many statues or idols, footprints and other holy deity mountains on the way along the pilgrimage circuit. Even today, one can see the mountain exactly as described and explained in the pilgrimage guide books or the scriptures. Less fortunate people can see it as a highly imposing mountain resembling a king sitting on his throne, and to its east lies the mountain called Po-nga-den as prophesied by Lord Buddha.

Mount Kailash is in between the range of five-peaked mountain and the Kunlun mountain range. As previously mentioned, this holy mountain attracts endless Buddhists,

Hindus, Jains and Bonpo pilgrims from Tibet and countries far and wide.

To the south is the palace of Goddess Saraswati called Menmo Nagnyil.

To the west is the Goddess Tara's pilgrimage site Riwotsegye.

To the north of Kailash is the palace of protector deities called Zawog Gurchen; other beings are like assembly of ministers in the Chamber of King's Court seated according to their portfolios, in a row having met with the King. We, thus, see the mountain in different visions depending on our karmic deeds.

Hindus consider the exterior of Mount Kailash to resemble a crystal stupa and its interior to be the abode of the Great Lord Shiva and his consort Uma Devi (Parvati), the daughter of the Himalaya. These pious Hindus consider the Kailash as the *swarg* or great throne of Lhachen Mahadeva, the Great Lord Shiva.

In 1948, Lama Govinda went with the principal objective of visiting the abandoned and vanished independent kingdom which once had its capital city of Tsarang located in the Upper Sutlej Valley to the south-west of Mount Kailash. He also had the aim of collecting old records of the temples and monasteries founded by Lotsawa Rinchen Sangpo. He made pilgrimages to Tibet and had a trip to Kailash. In his book, *The Way of the White Clouds*, Lama Anagarika Govinda elucidates the special high qualities of the sacred mountains. In the words of Lama Govinda, "some mountains are just mountains, but others are more, they have a personality, and hence the powers to influence people. When personality occurs in a human being, it can result in his becoming a great ruler or sage like the Buddha, when it occurs in a mountain, then it is recognized as a vessel of cosmic power and elevated to the status of a sacred mountain. There is never any need to point this out or argue the case, as it is usually quite obvious, and the sole response available is one of worship. To the truly spiritual man, the whole notion of climbing a sacred mountain would be utterly unthinkable. He would want to be conquered by the mountains rather than conquer the mountain himself. To achieve his goal, he will open himself to the mountain, contemplate it from every point of view and in all its moods and aspects, and thereby approach the very life of the mountain - a life that is as intense and varied as that of a human being. Mountains grow and decay, they breathe and pulsate with life. They attract and collect invisible energies from their surroundings".

As mentioned earlier, there are three pilgrimage circuits around Mount Kailash. The great Arhat (Foe-destroyers), god sand goddesses used the top one.

The hermits and the yogic practitioners take the middle circuit and the ordinary people take the outer circuit.

According to one sutra popularly known as Dophelmoche (མདོ་འཕལ་མོ་ཆེ), if one takes a single circumambulation of Mount Kailash one's accumulated demerits will be washed away. If one could circumambulate Thirteen times, all demerits accumulated in one own's lifetime will be purified, and one who could go 108 times around the mountain, will obtain the eight merits and become the renounced one.

This holy mountain has four gates and four immutable sacred nailing/(nails?) in the four directions. These gates and sacred nails support the permanent and immortal existence of Mount Kailash fixed by Lord Buddha himself along with his 500 disciples. In olden days, many holy and religious people spent their lives in this holy mountain by meditating either in the monasteries or inside the caves. When I say that Lord Buddha put four immutable sacred nails in the four directions of Mount Kailash, this does not mean that he travelled physically all the way from India to Kailash with his 500 disciples. He only made his holy trip to Mount Kailash along with his 500 disciples as a thin ray of light using his supernatural powers.

Although there are many pilgrimage sites in different parts of Tibet; Buddhists and Hindus of the Himalayan region of

India from Ladakh, Sikkim, Himachal Pradesh and other parts of India, Nepal and Bhutan used to prioritise making holy pilgrimages to Mount Kailash. A Tibetan person of western Tibet visits the Mount Kailash at least once in his lifetime without fail.

Today, everywhere in the world is getting closer and the name of the Mount Kailash is every one's talk in daily life; it has become a centre of attraction for tourists from all over the world. Its splendor, calm, cool and sacredness inspire people to know the reality of life. When the political situation remains calm, every year the number of pilgrims and trekkers to this holy mountain increases, and it has become the main source of income for both the government and individuals. The Chinese government expects a large number of pilgrims from Buddhist and Hindu countries including distinguished diplomats, travelers, explorers and keen geographers, nature-lovers and environmentalists or just tourists from all over the globe (with the exception of climbers). Every year, many people in western countries flock to Mount Kailash like a swarm of golden geese throughout the year except during winter. Many westerners visit Mount Kailash, especially during the Dharchen flag raising festival. For the convenience of western travelers and explorers who are eager to know more about the holy place of Mount Kailash and Lake Manasarovara, I want to write a brief note onhow to go around Mount Kailash, Lake Manasarovara including the holy, self-originated statues, caves, footprints on stone and other interesting sacred areas around the holy mountain and lake.

Commencing the outer circuit

For making ritual circumambulation around Mount Kailash or Gang Tise meaning "Cool Snow Mountain", there are two circuit routes for the pilgrims the inner and outer circuit. As mentioned earlier, most people circumambulate the latter thirteen times before proceeding to the former. Normally, people start their pilgrimage from the place known as Dharchen (in Tibetan) meaning, "Big prayer flagpole". This is the starting point for pilgrims to circumambulate the outer circuit. From here, Buddhists circumambulate in clock-wise direction, whereas the Bonpos circumambulate in an anti-clock wise direction.

Moving ahead farther, we first arrive at Chagtselkhang or Prostration place at the Lhalung's lower valley. It is said that Great Gyawa Gotsang Gonpo Dorjee discovered the outer pilgrimage circuit of Mount Kailash after visiting the Manasarovara Lake on the Lhado River. It was mid-day and the surrounding landscape was beautiful. He thought that he would take a rest and have lunch there because the place was very large. He went to collect three stones to male a hearth to prepare his meal. To his surprise, every stone he found had an image of a deity or sacred letters. He could not find even a single stone that could be used as a hearth stone. But he felt extremely happy and surprised to see these wonderful self-emanated inscriptions on the stones. Instead of preparing his meal, he offered prayers and continued his journey. Not far away, he saw the majestic crystal-clear Mount Kailash standing in front of him on the horizon of blue sky. On seeing it, his joy knew no bounds. He started paying respects and doing prostrations. So, that place came to be called (ཕྱག་འཚལ་སྐྱང་།) Chagtselkhang or Prostration Place.

After that name, people started their pilgrimage after doing a few prostrations here. They stood up and closed their eyes and bowed deeply to the sacred mountain. Complete silence prevailed over the area, and people were sincere in their salutation. The pilgrims were overawed by the overwhelming sanctity of the sacred mountain. People not only prostrated and prayed, but upon slowly opening their eyes, they stared up at the luminous peak, and they absorbed the holy mountain into their soul. They prayed that peace may prevail throughout the earth, and they also prayed for sentient beings living on this earth.

To the east of Chagtselkhang or Prostration House is the palace of Yellow Zambhala. If one goes a little farther, one arrives at a vast open ground called Serzhongthang meaning, "Golden Bowl Land". It is said that a very rich businessman provided a bowl full of gold to a poor man as a payment and asked him to circumambulate Mount Kailash as a pilgrim on his behalf. The poor man was so happy; he loaded the gold on the back of his donkey, and set out on pilgrimage on behalf of the rich man from Chagtselkhang. On reaching this vast open area, his donkey lay down and did not rise from the ground. When the poor animal's owner unloaded the bag of gold, the donkey got up, but on being re-laden the donkey sat down and refused to go ahead. As a result of this unusual incident, the poor man and the animal returned back to their starting place, because the man and the donkey could not circumambulate around Mount Kailash as wished by the rich man. On reaching the start, the man told the whole story to a holy saint who was living there. The holy saint told him that the rich businessman had earned money by cheating poor people, therefore, he had committed a sinful act, and the gifts of gold were not worth the value of offerings made by others for circumambulating around Mount Kailash. It was enough only for the value of the distance covered and he could not hope to complete the circuit around Mount Kailash. The poor man kept the full amount of gold for himself in the end, gold for himself, although he went only up to that place. Since then, the place has came to be known as Serzhongthang.

Raising the Big Flagpole at the foot of Mount Kailash

Dhar means flag (dhvaja) and Chen means big. So it is Dharpoche in local dialect. The big flag pole (Mahadhvaja) is hoisted. At the western foothills of the sacred mountain, the thrones of 500 Arhats (Foe-Destroyers) in the middle of Serzhongthang stands a lonely Ngari Dharchen at 4600 metres above sea level magnificent flag pole measuring approximately thirty metres tall. It has a diameter of 0.3 meters. This great prayer flagpole is made up of several trunks of pine trees strongly lashed end to end exactly like the mast of a sailing ship ; it is held up by ropes of untanned yak hide, still covered in hair. On this important day, the flagpole raising festival, it is completely festooned with bright new prayer flags. At its midpoint, four ropes of about two hundred meters each are attached; the ropes on four sides are entirely covered with prayer flags.

Allow me to tell you a little about this famous great prayer flagpole ceremoney. Every year, a big fair is held there on Vaishakha Shukla Chaturdasi and on every 15th of the 4th month of Tibetan Lunar calendar (full moon day in the month of May). This prayer flagpole - raising ceremony is held on this day in honour of Lord Buddha, to celebrate Saga Dawa. All the local heads of regions including nomadic headmen have to present themselves on this auspicious Dharchen ceremony. In the past the hoisting of the flagpole was entirely carried out by local Purang Taklakot people under the direct supervision of the Viceroy (Garpon) of Lhasa and the District Commissioner of Purang. If the Viceroys of Lhasa and commissioner were not able to attend the flagpole ceremony, they would send their special representatives to supervise the smooth hoisting of the big flagpole.

In olden days, the upper part the prayer flag Sertog and Gyaltsen of the religious victorious banner was prepared by the local government of Ngari. It was a woollen cloth to which were attached long cotton clothes printed with religious scripts that were from Lhasa. Every year, the Tse Lekhung of Lhasa sent a man with a strong horse direct from Lhasa to Mount Kailash with appropriate material for the prayer flag. The people of six villages of Purang carried out the raising and lowering of the huge flagpole and six people wrapped their arms and chest by woollen cloths with seal of district office. The full moon day of 15th Saga Dawa is very important day in our religious calendar, as it is the day of birth, enlightenment and mahaparinirvana day of Lord Buddha. It is also said that on the same day, Lord Buddha and his 500 followers also visited the holy Mount Kailash during his lifetime, and came there flying like birds and began to sit perched on the four sides of the Mount Kailash. It is also believed that Lord Buddha preached kLubum) teachings to the serpent-king Mado and composed the Lankavatara Sutra on that very day.As per Gangri Karchak from page 60 it is stated in below.

Every twelve years, a big trade fair is held on this particular day. During the heyday of the Guge Kingdom, so many Buddhist teachings were translated into Tibetan. When Buddhism was at its peak period of spreading into Tibet, Pandit Somnath of Kashmir translated the Kalachakra Jyotisha into Tibetan in 1027. From this day onward, the Brihaspati cycle of sixty years called Rab-byung (Prabhava) was introduced. The cycle of sixty years was further divided into five sub-cycles of twelve years each. The Talo or Horse year in the seventh year of the cycle is considered as the auspicious date to perform parikrama at Mount Kailash.

The Buddhist Annals tells us that only a man entirely free from sin could climb the Mount Kailash. Such a person wouldn't have to actually scale the sheer walls of ice to do the hard works, as the modern mountaineers have to do. He would just turn himself into a bird and fly to the summit through the rays of sun.

A person especially appointed by the District Commissioner of Purang brought down the old prayer flag on the 13th. With the old flags taken off, the person would begin to hang newly sewn flags and Khatas on the flagpole and officials inspected the flagpole area. People used to tie their own offerings including Khatas to the holy flagpole. Once the elegant flag pole an entirely new look, the Chairperson would give the command to the 14th of 4th Tibetan month (Saga Dawa) position the newly decorated flagpole at an angle or half-raised with the tip of the pole facing north towards Choeku Monastery in order to allow it to pay respect to the monastery for a night. And so it lay with its base adjacent to a big hole at the centre of a mound of stones.

དེ་མ་ཐག་རྒྱ་གར་འཕགས་པའི་ཡུལ་ནས་སྤྱོན་པ་བཙམ་ལྡན་འདས་ལྟ་བུ་ཕྱུབ་པ་འཁོར་དགྲ་བཙམ་པ་ལུ་བརྒྱ་དང་བཅས་པ་དང་བའི་རྒྱལ་པོ་བཞིན་ནས་མཁན་ལ་འཕུར་ནས་སྐྱད་ཅིག་གིས་ཕེབས་ཏེ། དེ་སེའི་ནུབ་ཕྱོགས་དཀྱིལ་འཁོར་སྟེང་ཞེས་པའི་བྲག་སྟེང་དུ་དགྲ་བཙམ་ལུ་བརྒྱ་དང་བཅས་པ་བབས་ནས་ཞབས་རྗེས་རེ་བཞག་པ། དེ་སེ་ཕྱོགས་བཞི་ལ་དེ་སེ་མི་འགྱུར་བའི་གཟེར་ཆེན་བཞི་ཞེས་གྲགས་པར་ཞབས་རྗེས་བཞག། ལང་ཀཱ་ཕུ་རང་གི་རི་ཉེར་བཞུགས་ནས་བྱང་རྒྱབ་སེམས་དཔའ་རྩྭ་གྲོལ་ཆེན་པོས་ཞེས་ནས་ལང་གར་གཞེགས་པའི་མདོ་གསུངས་ཅེས་གསལ།

In the olden days, on the early morning of the 15th day of Saga Dawa, the Khenpo of the Choeku Monastery led the function of performing prayers along with the monks. Strong people were divided into four groups as pullers and pushers.

In each group, there were about a hundred people. The former pulled the rope from its four directions accordingly, while the latter operated V-shaped operated with lifting levers made of wood.

The final hoisting ceremony proceeded by stages, according to a recital of prayers. A group of monks with new maroon robes and wearing red hats blew traditional giant alpine horns and conches, with clashing big cymbals and drums banging. The head lama with other monks loudly chanted prayers and performed rituals with perfect hand gestures in exquisite unison. From the giant incense fires, the surrounding area was fully filled with a sweet fragrant air and the circumambulators swirled round and round. The people held prayer flags and either bowed their heads to the flags or touched them to their brows. At last, the lead lama raised his hand with a loud voice and gave the command.

The senior Mayor (fully attired in traditional Tibetan costume) of the six villages bowed his head thrice with a cap in his hand and gave order to people to raise the flagpole and flag. The pullers pulled and the pushers pushed with their cross poles with great shouts of, "Shao chig maagnyis" (like "one, two, three!"). The pullers' rope went taut, the lifting levers were jostled into place, and the great pole jerked into life without any difficulty and Dharchen rose up straight on its own. The spectators standing around the surrounding places gave big shout Lha-so- so! Lha-so-so! As the great flagpole rose, longer braces were positioned to support it in between the pulls. The head of the team with his assistants made adjustments from four directions and to the strength of the pulls. It is very important that Dharchen should sink into its foundation at exactly the right angle. The Dharchen must stand vertical. It is believed that if the Dharchen tilts in the slightest degree in any direction, great disasters and ill-fortune will follow for the whole of Tibet for the twelve months. All people gathered there with great excitement on these days tied their own small prayer flags to any of the four side ropes.

More incense and tsampa with butter were put into the burning fire to make sure that a huge amount of smoke should rise from it. Finally, the whole population gathered around the newly dressed giant flagpole, and as part of the rite performed by the leader of monks, the people threw up handsfuls of tsampa three times in the air. Everybody assembled at the function used to shout, "Lha Gyalo!" "Victory to God!".

The monks of Choeku Monastery would progress around the prayer flagpole along with their ritual prayer implements and the spectators swarmed down to join the circumambulation. During this time, the whole area appeared to be one united massive swirling whirlpool of dust, color and excitement. People forgot all wordly miseries and sorrows. They prayed to the sacred mountain for proper protection, peace in the land and healthy life and prosperity for individuals as well the whole community. After completing hoisting the prayer flag, the great swirl began to disperse and break up into small groups. Some of the pilgrims queued up for hours prostrate themselves. Some people held khatas, in their hands and placing it against their head for some time, looked towards Dharchen first and then to Mount Kailash then bent their heads down with folded hands and prayed for a few minutes and wrapped the scarves around their necks. They visualised they had received blessings and scarves from the gods and the deities of Mount Kailash. Many of them placed their heads briefly against the trunk of the newly hoisted Dharchen to ensure that they made direct contact with the life force with which it was now imbued.

Presently those who wish to circumambulate continue their journey from here around Mount Kailash. The Dharchen (flagpole) hoisting event marks the beginning of the new year for circumambulating around Mount Kailash. People at Dharchen are in holiday mood, with smiling faces and dressed in new clothes with valuable ornaments. Those who are lovers of dance join hands and start to dance. A few people begin singing and many of them return to their tents, laughing and shouting cheerfully at each other with joy. On this day, as I have said before, circumambulation is open for the pilgrims, so people proceed on their journey.

In olden days, this event was organised as purely an official festival, so the people gathered on this day were mostly male, because they were representing each of the nomads, villages and towns of the Ngari, some women attended with their husbands and families. Not many pilgrims attended in those early days.

Now things have changed and the situation is completely different. On this particular day thousands of people of different ages gather here from different countries. Coming from isolated communities, this is a very rare opportunity for younger members of the population. They will see thousands of young faces from far and near. A great feeling of community sharing arises. Like in the old days, the young male population start to sing to the female population a song called mZa'-glu (མཛའ་གླུ) and females reply either the negative or positive. In the old days, there was no alcohol, but now gifts of drinks, food and presents are given on this day. This is a great festival, and one must not miss the chance visit it once in one's lifetime.

The Victory Flagpole

❖

There is a story related to the prayer flag hoisted during the reign of His Holiness the fifth Dalai Lama. Miwang Gaden Tsewang, was a army general of the Tibetan army, appointed by His Holiness the Fifth Dalai Lama in 1679. Gaden Tsewang led an army expedition in Ngari against the army of Ladakh army. Ladakh had invaded Ngari in 1633 under the command of the Namgyal dynasty of Ladakh had defeated the Guge Kingdom. The last king of the Guge dynasty Tri Dakpa Tashi was either killed or taken as a prison to Ladakh. When the Guge Kingdom was captured by Ladakh, thousand of people were killed along with its ministers and the members of the royal family. The Namgyal dynasty of Ladakh ruled over Ngari from 1633 to 1679 CE. King Gelek Namgyal of Ladakh extended his jurisdiction towards U-Tsang and there were a number of skirmishes between Ngari-Ladakh and U-Tsang at the border around Sangsang. These small skirmishes at last led to a full-fledged war between the two Buddhist neighbouring countries. Desi Lobsang Jinpa resigned from the post of regent and Sangay Gyatso succeeded as the regent of the Fifth Dalai Lama. He consulted His Holiness and decided to send massive armed forces towards Ngari. This was his military expansion for setting the political boundary of Gaden Podrang.

When Gaden Tsewang, who was a nephew of Tenzin Choegyal, a Mongol general, was appointed as the commander of the Tibetan army in 1679 to lead the military expedition toward Ngari, first he fought a number of small engagements with Ladakh right at the border of Ngari in Tripa County of

Saga district in the lower part of the Ngari region. In every engagement, Ladakh had lost until Gaden Tsewang and his armed force reached Mount Kailash.

The Ladakh army retreated to hold major important areas like old forts and monasteries in upper part of Ngari. It was very difficult for Gaden Tsewang to drive them completely away because Ladakh sent reinforcements. Although Gaden Tsewang had 25,000 calvalry with him to fight the enemy, it was too hard for him to drive out the enemy from the territories of Ngari.

General Gaden Tsewang made a request to the Lhasa Government for more reinforcements from Lhasa that would enable him to make a final assault against Ladakh. General Gaden Tsewang knew that it was good to make prayers at Mount Kailash and make the goddess of Kailash happy and also to seek protection from the deities of Mount Kailash. He along with his army generals and army performed a big prayer on the 15th day of Saga Dawa of Iron Bird in year (1681 CE) and hoisted a big prayer flag and burnt incense on this particular day. Lord Buddha was born, and attained enlightenment on this day, and it is our irrefutable belief and faith that on this particular day Lord Buddha along with his 500 disciples visited and blessed the spot where he left his footprints which we call immutable sacred nails on the four sides of Mount Kailash. As reinforcement, another 25,000 cavalry arrived from Lhasa. Gaden Tsewang made final assaults against the enemy, and he very easily annihilated the enemy's army. Gaden Tsewang considered that his prayers and flag hoisting at Mount Kailash increased his fortune and that the deities of Mount Kailash had rewarded his good service. Gaden Tsewang returned to Ngari in 1682 from Leh, Ladakh after capturing the enemy capital. He celebrated his victory over Ladakh and again on the same day, he hoisted the big prayer flag on the same site on which he had hoisted it a year ago. He called it a victory prayer flag. From then on, Gaden Tsewang regarded this flag as very important and he attached special importance to the hoisting of this particular prayer flag at Mount Kailash.

The hoisting of the prayer flag at the Mount Kailash is very famous, and we Ngariwas consider this as a victory flagpole standing against the evil and also consider it as a dignified pillar protecting of peace and tranquility in Tibet as a whole. This hoisting of the prayer flag is a very important religious festival all the world, and Ngari people in particular.

Firstly, it is very important for the Buddhist people and for prosperity and peace in the world as a whole.

Secondly, it supports the spirit of the people of Snowland and Buddhism, and the well-being of all entire sentient beings.

Thirdly, it has special religious significance and importance for the people of Ngari as a whole.

Fourthly, it supports our wish that evil times may not come again. As Ngari say: that the demons may not come again until the snow mountains have melted away and the oceans have dried up. So everyone wishes that evil times might not come again to the Land of Snow.

Fifthly, it is famous because people recognise the Ngari prayer flag hoisting and its religious ceremony. The day of the prayer hoisting ceremony is also considered as meeting of deities and human beings at Dharchen at the throne of the Arhats (foe-destroyers) on the foothill of Mount Kailash. This day is also called the opening day of Mount Kailash because that is when the general public take part in ritual walking around the sacred Mount Kailash to benefit their own lives.

In earlier time, Tibetans from various western regions, and a few Hindus, come to Mount Kailash on this auspicious day. During the Cultural Revolution, the flagpole was not spared but was completely destroyed. People could not perform the holy prayer flag hoisting ceremony. After many years with some relaxation on religious activities by the Chinese authorities, the people of Western Tibet started hoisting small prayer flags on the old site in 1983. Later, authorities gave them permission to raise this particular prayer flag on the same day, as per the rules laid down by the relevant authorities.

Today western people call it the Dharchen festival, and there are so many western and other tourists attending the event. This festival is the main attraction of the year for tourists and of great historical significance also.

In Chinese-occupied Tibet, Mount Kailash has become the main tourist attraction and also the main source of income for both the government and the local people. Thousands of western and eastern people gather there to watch the festival with much gaiety and excitement. The Purang valley is still the gateway to this holy place, and the entire Tibetan people of western Tibet uniquely manage these activities with great faith and devotion.

Just above Dharchen, there is the huge sacred rocky throne-like platform that is said to be the throne of 500 Arhats (Foe-Destroyers). It is believed that when Lord Buddha with his 500 disciples were staying at Gaya, a demon called Gonpo Ben who was living in Lanka Lake (Rakshas Tal) tried to take this holy Mount Kailash to his place, by putting a rope around Mount Kailash to take it on his back. Through a holy vision, Lord Buddha visualized the demon Gonpo Ben's heinous intention to take the Mount Kailash to his place, which would have been unfortunate. Lord Buddha and his followers at once flew towards the Mount Kailash like a flock of geese. Lord Buddha and 500 disciples blessed this holy Mount Kailash from four directions. They flew and sat on the rocks and left footprints on the rock. Since then, this event is called the Mount Kailash's immutable sacred nailing for the benefit of human beings living on this earth. Even today, the footprints of Lord Buddha and his disciples can be seen at the site. Charles Allen (1982) in his book says for human beings this is a gateway to heaven, "This area overlooking Dharchen is a flat shelf of rock rather like the deck of a giant aircraft carrier which juts out over the valley", but we consider this flat rock shelf is merely the transit space.

We generally call the place of Arhats' (Foe-Destroyers) Burial Ground (དགྲ་བཅོམ་སྐུ་རྒྱུའི་དུར་ཁྲོད།). Here lies the cemetery of Eighty-four Mahasiddhas (Great Accomplished beings). The sky burial site is considered one of the most auspicious and holiest burial sites among the holy cemetery grounds in Tibet. We don't know when or who first started sky burial here for the first time. Bonpos have been there for many centuries, while the Kagyupa sect established their supremacy in the twelfth century only. This burial ground rock platform and the surrounding caves and rock shelter were a favorite meditation location for the Bon yogis and great teachers for many years. Later on, the Bon yogis disappeared from Mount Kailash, and it was then solely used by Kagyudpa hermits (ripas).

Holy Places near by

❖

If we go little further, at the edge of this huge rocky ground, we will find a cave known as Naro Bonchung's cave; to one side of it, there is Milarepa's footprint.

A little spring flows under the rock cave. This water is considered to have healing and curing power for miserable diseases. A little above this place is a stupa resembling the rocky mountain at the edge, and there are self-emanated statues of the Sixteen Great Arhats (Foe-Destroyers). Towards the west while crossing the Lhachu River and north of Golden Valley, there is the high clay-mountain called Zamnak, the Palace of Black Jambhala. To its right side on a rocky place, there is a cave of Guru Padmasambhava called Sa-ngak Choephug (gSang-sngags Chos-phug) along with many other caves, with holy waters brought forth by Guru Rinpoche. There are also his hand print and footprint. There are deities of Four Tantras on the rocky mountain, and there are self-emanated statues of Lord Avalokiteshvara on the top, and his two disciples and Lord Khasarpani. To its left towards the north stands a huge mountain called Zawog Gurkhang, the abode of deities of Mount Kailash.

Just below this lofty and gigantic mountain, there is a cave called Richen Cave. It is from this cave that Milarepa entered into his mystical magical contest with Naro Bonchung. When Milarepa arrived at Mount Kailash and while making his circumambulation of the mountain, he encountered Naro Bonchung at this very place. Naro Bonchung insisted to Milarepa, "You and I should have a trial of strength". Naro

Bonchung immediately lifted a huge stone about the size of a yak. Milarepa was not at all intimidated by the performance of his opponent; Milarepa lifted both rock and lifter. Milarepa was still not satisfied with this trial of strength but sat himself in the Lotus Cave on the western side of Lhalung (Valley of God). At that time, Naro Bonchung was meditating in his cave on the east side of Lhalung. Milarepa stretched his one leg straight across to the mouth of a cave on the east side near Naro Bonchung's cave. Naro Bonchung tried to perform the same kind of feat but he failed to do so. It is said this feat caused great laughter among the lha and lha ma yin (gods and demi-gods) watching from the sky.

It was Milarepa's second defeat of Naro Bonchung at this very cave. There are many caves around Milarepa's cave and these small caves on the hills and rocky mountains are generally known as bird shelter or nest (བྱ་ཚང་།). These caves belonged to the Shri Drugpa Kagyud School.

Just below this holy cave and mountain, there is a monastery called Nyenpo Rizong, named by the great religious saint and hermit Nyenpo Rizong who founded the monastery. The ruins of this old monastery can be seen here even to this day. A new monastery has been built and named as Choeku Monastery. Khan Nyanpo Drubchen and followers of Dogon Tsangpa Gyare built this famous monastery. The main holy statue in this monastery is Choeku Wopakme. Hence, it is named Choeku Monastery. The religious sect of this monastery is Drukpa Kagyud and is financed and managed by Lho Drukpa. A eulogy to the monastery and its main image says;

Turning the Wheel of Dharma in the Land of Joy,
Always keeps sentient beings in compassionate vision,
Treated equally the oath and commitment,
Salute and praise to such a pure meditator"

In the past, five self-emanated marble stone images of Lord Avalokiteshvara were found near the Milk Lake in Garsha region, the land of the goddess in Himachal Pradesh, India. These statues were considered to be brothers. Later, they came to be kept in different locations;

1. Garsha Phakpa in Garsha Monastery, Kulu District, Himachal Pradesh, India

2. Tang Phakpa in Guge Monastery, Tsarang District in Ngari, Tibet

3. Tradun Namlha Karpo on the bank of Martsang Tsangpo in Tradun, Drongpa District in Ngari, Tibet

4. Kyunglung Opame in Dawa District in Ngari, Tibet

5. Choeku Wodpakme in Nyenpo Rizong Monastery at Mount Kailash.

Garsha Phakpa can be seen today in the same monastery, where Choeku Wodpakme is, which was rebuilt in 1986. three other statues were lost during the dark days of the Cultural Revolution whose perpetrators' aim was demolishing the monasteries.

The Choeku Wodpakme statue has its own legend regarding the way it came to Mount Kailash in Western Tibet. During the glorious reign of the sixth King Choegyal Tsede of the Guge dynasty, a holy hermit from Garsha region offered the statue to the king. For a long period, it remained in the Guge Kingdom. One fine day, the protector-deities of Mount Kailash, disguised as seven Indian yogis, came to Guge asking for alms in the temple where this holy statue was kept. The monks in the monastery in Guge Kingdom mistreated them instead of giving alms and food. The seven yogis immediately turned into wolves and vanished. Exactly seven days after this incident, the Mount Kailash protector-deities have took away Choeku Wodpakme from the Guge monastery to Nyenpo Rizong monastery. The caretaker of the Nyenpo Rizong monastery could not discover who had installed the idol in the monastery that night. The devotees of that temple, however, regarded it as a gift from the deities and venerated it with deep respect and warm regard.

For many years, the king of Guge could not find out where the holy statue had gone and who had stolen it from his monastery. It only later during the reign of Chogyal Tri Dakpa Tashi that the king of Guge came to know that the holy statue was at Nyenpo Rizong in Mount Kailash. He dispatched an army to bring it back to the Kingdom of Guge, waging a war against the monastery, during which Guge took many holy articles from Choeku Monastery. The holy image was so heavy that the Guge army could not take it easily, and dragged it up to the Palace of Zamnak. As the army could not move the idol any further, the soldiers decided to break it into pieces and re-assemble it back in Guge Kingdom. However, when one of the powerful men hit a chisel with hammer on the right knee of the image, suddenly the image spoke out, "Oh! You Sinner, it is too painful". The armed forces of Guge were astounded to see that a lifeless stone image was uttering words. They left the statue where it was and ran back to their kingdom. Among the holy articles that the Guge army had taken away to Guge Kingdom, there were two wonderful brass cooking utensils known as Tsogkhro. One day, when the monks of Guge Kingdom were making tea in these two pots, the tea turned into blood and the monks became superstitious, thinking it a bad omen for the monastery as well as for the whole kingdom. While the boiling tea in the pot flew back to Nyenpo Rizong from Guge Kingdom, falling upon the high mountains. Later on, the mountains became popularly known as Red Tea Mountain (ཇ་ རེ་དམར་པོ།)

A history record, *Gangri Karchag Shelkyi Melong* (Gangsri dKarchag Shel-gyi Melong) says that, a few days after this incident, the cook of the Nyenpo Rizong Monastery went to fetch dried yak dun for fuel for cooking. He found the statue in the rocky mountain, and the statue told the cook to carry him on his back along with the dried yak-dung. The cook replied that when such strong armed forces could not move the statue, it would be very difficult for him to do so. When the statue insisted that the cook should do this, the cook replied that he will take out the dried yak-dung from his basket and then would happily carry the statue. The holy statue replied that it was not necessary to take out the dried dung, but rather place it on top of the basketful of dung. The holy image was so light that it weighed no more heavy than a tree leaf on his back. The man proceeded to the monastery, but when he arrived just below Nyenpo Rizong monastery, the statue became heavy, and he left it there by itself. Later on, a new monastery was built on this site.

This monastery had its own unique beauty in its collection of holy images. Choeku Wodpakme is the main image and is placed in the center. It is the symbol of the Buddha's body; its image of Naropa is the symbol of Buddha's speech; and the big image of Tsogkhro is the symbol of Buddha's mind. Other images, like a Buddha image made of which is said once to have spoken, were offered by Drukpa Ralung monastery is also a gilded brass image of Lord Manjushri, an image of Padmasambhava, an image of Lord Buddha, an image of Drogon Tsangpa Gyare and an image of Milarepa. There were also Kagyur texts and images of Shabtrung Ngawang Namgyal and others. The protector-deity of the monastery is Tise Lhatsen, a powerful jakme; the monastery has separate houses for these deities. This monastery was owned by the Drukpa Kagyud sect and founded by Nyenpo Drubchen and Drogon Tsangpa Gyare. The exact date and the year of its construction cannot be found, as the old records of the monastery were lost during the so-called Cultural Revolution.

Like all the monasteries in Chinese-occupied Tibet, all the thirteen monasteries around the Mount Kailash and Manasarovara Lake including Choku Wodpakme fell captive to the Red Guards, and were not spared during the Cultural Revolution. Some of them were completely demolished, and no-one will see their like or grandeur again. In early 1980s, the Chinese government relaxed its policy to religion a little during which the Tibetans reconstructed most of these monasteries, but not in their original shape or grandeur.

The reconstruction Choeku Monastery was completed in the year 1985 and its inauguration was celebrated on the 15th day of Saga Dawa the same year. Now, anyone who wishes can visit and receive blessings from Choeku Opame when they make their pilgrimage to Mount Kailash.

After almost two decades, the holy statue of Choeku Wodpakme was reinstalled in its monastery.

Let me tell you the story of how this holy image was spared during the Cultural Revolution and kept safe and sound.

During the days of the Cultural Revolution, destruction was carried out by the Chinese to meticulously annihilate the very existence of Tibet within Tibet. One of the faithful residents of the monastery took the statue from the monastery secretly. He hid it on the bank of Lake Manasarovara with the hope that one day the younger generation and followers of Buddhism would rebuild the Choeku Monastery and would require the statue. They could then reinstall it as the central statue of the monastery as in the past. With the passage of time, however, nothing happened. The statue's rescuer was getting old and sick, but fearing that the holy image might be destroyed, he did not tell anyone about it. Luckily, the monk had a loyal disciple who was living amongst the general public. So a few days before his death, the monk told his disciple about the holy image and its location. He advised his disciple to keep it secret until better days. During the relaxation of religious restrictions in Tibet, devotees living in the Ngari rebuilt this monastery with their own funds. As per directions given by his late teacher, the disciple disclosed the statue's secret to other people and they left for Lake Manasarovara. They found the holy image facing toward the Mount Kailash, and it was as fresh as it was in the monastery almost two decades ago. The idol was been taken to the monastery, and it is safe and secure in the monastery today.

A little way beyond the Choeku Monastery toward the south, there is a cave called Garuda, and in this cave, we can see a self-emanated figure of Garuda. The mountain in which the cave is formed is also shaped like Garuda. Near this cave, there are seven birth's holy waters. Below this monastery, there is a big protruding rock, known as an abode of Maitreya. Just near to it, there are footprints of Goddess Tara and a holy cave called Langchen Belphuga located at an elephant-shaped sacred mountain. It is said that Guru Padmasambhava hid treasure in this cave.

In the Padma bka'-thang, it is written that,

"Guru Rinpoche had subdued 28 goddesses, the moving stars believed to be daughters of the four guardian kings of the world or the constellation (རྒྱུ་སྐར་ཉི་ཤུ་རྩ་བརྒྱད།) at "Gangs Tise".

He had hidden a treasure of sacred texts inside this cave for the benefit of people in the near future. Pilgrims cannot only to visit the caves but also look at the ruins of the monasteries in Ngari. Apparently, major Buddhist ruins are found in Ngari, created during the invasion by Ladakh and the 50 years rule by the Ladakhi kings under the Namgyal Dynasty of Ladakh in early 17th century.

Near Langchen Belphug, there is a spring, said to come from Lake Manasarovara, which is also regarded as a source of holy water for eliminating obscurations of oneself and others.

At a little distance from Mount Kailash, there is the cave known as Lotus Cave (པདྨ་ཕུག) and beside it, there is a flat stone like a holy scripture, and on this flat stone falls the holy spring of nectar. If one proceeds a little upward towards the Mount Nyenri Zatrin Yanyin range, one will see the three peaks as if touching the sky. They are regarded as the Three Goddesses of Long Life -"ཚེ་ལྷ་རྣམ་གསུམ།". The first range is Goddess Tara's abode, while the middle one is Tse-pagme's abode shaped as holy nectar vase, and the third mountain is called Tsugtor Namgyalma's abode, and it is shaped as a stupa.

Just next to these three mountains are seven lofty mountains. We find three different accounts of these holy mountains. Some people believe that these mountains are the palaces of Seventy-five Dharma Protectors while others believe that they represent the (sGrubchen brgyad cu) palaces of the Eighty Great Indian Ascetics or Great Buddhist Saints (སྒྲུབ་ཆེན་ བརྒྱད་ཅུ). Still others believe that they represent the Great Ling Gesar Gyalpo surrounded by his father and six brothers. At the western side of these mountains, there is a small but beautiful valley, containing holy cave of Baiphuk Sangwa Bhumchu, the meditation cave of Deity Eka Jati.

After crossing Lhachu (River of the God) from Nyenpo Rizong, and moving a little further to the cliff of the mountain, one will see a rainbow-like spring flowing downward. This is called holy water of Mount Kailash. Next to this area, there are some cliff mountains with very sharp-pointed peaks as if peering towards the sky. The Tibetan people believe that this mountain is the abode of Gonpo Ben and the protector-deity. The cliffs are said to be Gonpo's sacred offering of the ritual cakes (གཏོར་མ།) with his yak and his dog.

At the ridge of those mountains, there is an imposing rocky mountain called Monkey Holding Incense. The top of this mountain is flat. According to our mythology, the Monkey-king Hanuman sliced off its peak and took it away to cure the sick Lakshmana of the Ramayana epic. We regard this mountain as a medicinal mountain, because it is the source of a variety of medicinal herbs for healing sick people. In the middle of these mountains and just below the Dolma Pass, there is a holy nectar lake. Next to this lake, there is a sort of milky water falling down from a white, cow-shaped like rock.

It is believed that this water fulfills the wishes of all the sentient beings. On the other side of Monkey Holding Incense Mountain rock, there is a white stone resembling a glass marble frame where the great saint Nyeolha Nang (Nyonlha Nangpa?) had a vision of Avalokiteshvara vanishing inside the white stone resembling a glass marble frame. Some people say that it is a divination dice of Great Ling Gesar, the legendary king known as the manifestation of Lord Avalokiteshvara.

At the western side of those mountains, there is the abode of Tara and from there a very spring dashes through the high mountain cliffs, like horse tails moved by the wind; it has aptly been called the tail of Ta Kyangpo. Below this holy spring, if you go further, you will find clean and clear water falling into a rocky cave, known as the Milking Pot of Drukmo, the queen of Ling Gesar. To the west of this area, there is a stone boulder on the roadside as big as a Tibetan yak tent. It is called Queen Drukmo's Rolling Stone.

By proceeding a little further and from the eastern road side of Gonpo's ritual-cake mountain, one can glimpse holy Mount Kailash and a small mountain adjacent to it. This small snowy mountain, Little Kailash, is called the son of the Mount Kailash. This is also known as the Western Gate Chagtsalkhang, where people conduct prayers. Near this area, two big stones are said to be the Queen Drukmo's Handloom Stones (འབྲུག་མོའི་ ཐགས་རྫ). Tibetan ladies use such stones for weaving woollen cloth (སྣམ་བུ). If one climbs up, in the middle of an open area, we find a tiny but beautiful place popularly known as Tadin guest house and a self-emanated figure of Lhudul Pawo Tadin along with the footprints of Lord Buddha and his 500 disciples, the Western Side Immutable Nail.

One will come across there a glass-like door having boulders resembling four guards. On the outer pilgrimage circuit, there is a Tibetan letter "ཨ" said to have been written on the rock by Nyingmapa's Siddha (saint) Dongtul Gyawa with his forefinger.

It is important as well as interesting to know about Driraphuk Monastery. Gyawa Gotsang Gonpo Dorje was the pioneer who discovered the circumambulatory route around Mount Kailash and Manasarovara Lake while he was on his way to Mount Kailash to open a new pilgrimage circumambulatory route for ordinary people. When he reached there, he found a wonderful valley, and seeing a mountain, he learned that this beautiful lofty mountain is an abode of one thousand Buddhas. He thought that this mountain should also be put within the circumambulatory pilgrimage route, and he proceeded towards that mountain. All of a sudden, a female wild yak or drongdrima appeared in front of him. He was surprised to see the appearance of the animal, which he visualized the manifestation of Snowlion-Faced Sky-Walker (སེང་གེ་མོ་གདོང་མ།) who had appeared in disguise to show him the path. Since then, the valley has been known as the valley of the wild yak (འབྲོང་ལུང་།) as it was named first by Gyawa Gotsangpa because there were a plenty of wild yak or drong in the upper part of the valley. The animal encountered by Gyawa Gotsangpa went towards the east and he followed the animal; on reaching the corner of a cave, the 'drong' vanished. The monk looked all around. But there was no sign of the animal at all. The Drong was nowhere to be found.

He climbed up on a rock and looked around the area, whereupon he saw footprints of the same animal on the rock (which still existed in 1959, so must be there today). He saw the prints of the horn of the animal, as it miraculously entered into the rock. Because of the clear print of the horn of the animal on the rocks, this place came to be known as Drithim Driraphuk (Female Wild Yak Disappearance and her Horn-marked Cave). He saw this as an indication from holy deities that he should spend some time to meditate and do retreats in this cave. He climbed above the cave to have a glimpse of the place. The footprint was present on the rocks and he found it a perfect area to spend some time doing meditation. He repaired the cave with stones, constructing walls on the side of the rock to make it suitable for accommodation, and spent some time there. Sengdongma or Snowlion-Faced Sky-Walker supplied food to Gyawa Gotsang Gonpo Dorje a beautiful Valley above the present Drithim Driraphuk Monastery, a place that came to be known as Gang Khyam.

Gyawa Gotsang Gonpo Dorjee first arrived at Mount Kailash in 1212 and spent five years there. In 1217, when the warm days were about to end and the chilly winter days were approaching, Gotsang Gonpo Dorjee thought that the weather was uncongenial and the food was scarce, and it was time for him to leave this area and conclude his meditation, have successfully opened up the new route to Mount Kailash for the ordinary people. Prior to leaving the cave, he prayed that all living beings including the birds and insects who touched it with their head may not reborn in the lower samsaric realms. Instead, they may be reborn in the heaven realms. He leaned his head forward with folded hands and touched the sides of the cave, and there appeared a self-print of his head. While he was coming out from this small cave, his hat touched the upper part of the rock again and the print of his hat appeared there. There were also his footprints on the rock of the cave which existed until 1959. Surely they are still there. Once Gyawa Gotsangpa commenced meditation practice in that place, it was continued by followers of the Kadgudpa sect of hermits.

Drubchen Kyapgon Gangri Tsencen, a great Drukpa Kagyud Lama, after visiting the holy place got the impression that the land is very holy and was an auspicious place to build a monastery. Thus, he built a monastery called Driraphuk Gonpa named after Driraphuk cave. The religious sect of this monastery is Drukpa Kagyu. The Drukpa Kagyud sect of Dingche Dhondup Thongmon monastery financed and managed this monastery till 1959. During the Cultural Revolution in Tibet under the alien Chinese rule, many of the monasteries in Tibet were destroyed and demolished beyond recognition of their formal existence. This monastery was also completely destroyed. There was nothing left, and all the writings and priceless holy artifacts were totally burnt or taken to Beijing. The monastery was rebuilt in 1986 with financial help from the religious people of Ngari.

This elegant mountain that lies behind this monastery is the palace of One Thousand Buddhas.

According to the praise of Demchok,

> Mount Tise is Sengdong Karmo (Seng-gDong dKar-mo), the place of body (Rupa),
> The south side is Tagdong Karmo (sTag-gDong bKar-mo), the place of speech,
> In lower Kongpo and Tsari, the Phagdong Nagmo (Phag-gDong Nagmo), the place of mind.

Driraphuk Monastery is situated just below the holy place of Sengdongma (Snowlion-faced Sky-Walker) on the left side of Lhachu River. Although this monastery is very small compared to other monasteries, its fame is widespread throughout Tibet. It is well known for its unique beautiful location, and the holy mountain serves as the backdrop to the monastery. It is also the first meditation area of Gyalwa Gotsangpa.

A great hermitage known as Drubchok Mipham Yongdul's meditation cave is in the middle of this holy mountain. On the upper part of the mountain, there is an idol of Guru Rinpoche riding a pig; with the rein of pig is in the hands of a demoness. At the beautiful Gang Khyam valley, there is a spring called Silver Vase known as the Palace of serpent king Tsugna Rinchen. Behind this mountain, one can see three elegant lofty mountains, symbolizing the Three Great Buddhist Deities, that is, Avalokiteshvara (སྤྱན་རས་གཟིགས།), Manjushri (འཇམ་དཔལ་དབྱངས།) and Vajrapani (ཕྱག་ན་རྡོ་རྗེ།).

Towards the north of Mount Kailash, there are three majestic holy peaks considered to represent Gonpo Jarog Dongcen (Crow-faced Protector-deity). There are clear footprints of five groups of mkha'-'Dro (Sky-Walkers) on this mountain.

If one proceeds a little further from Driraphuk Monastery, one will come across a rock known as Crow Guest House (བྱ་

རྡོ་མརྒྱན་ཁང་) which is only a short only a trip from Khando-sanglam chu in the east. The story of that one day in the morning when Gotsangpa was offering gTorma or ritual cake (གཏོར་མ) to the goddess of the Tsewalung at the place where he had meditated a number of months and discovered the circuit route of Lake Manasarovara and on his way to Mount Kailash, a crow came and took away his plate of ritual cake (གཏོར་མ). As he followed the crow, the crow disappeared in the rock and he was very much surprised. He wanted to know what it really indicated. He found out that it was a protector-deity who had come to show him the path to Mount Kailash. This crow left the imprint of his body on the rock can be seen on the circuit route, as mentioned in the Guide Book of Kailash.

These days, however, if one climbs up from Nyentsong Jonggyud one can see the imprint of the crow on the rock at the site. When visiting, one should not miss seeing the footprints of the Great Masters and holy deities while circumambulating the outer circuit of Mount Kailash. One should not miss to have a holy glimpse of footprints of Goddess Tara on the flat stone. Little away from it, one should not miss seeing the footprints of Goddess Tara on the flat stone, and further on, more footprints of Goddess Tara imprinted on the rock.

Below this of Tara on rock, there is a big, famous burial ground called Sipatsal (bsil-pa-tsal, བསིལ་བ་ཚལ). Above this burial place, there is yet another footprint of Drigung Kagyud's great hermit Drubthob Gyawa Nyonlha who was one of the greatest hermits; he spent a number of years at Mount Kailash spreading his teachings. He was also a great religious teacher, practitioner and reformer of the Drigung Kagyud Sect. His footprint is very clear; it is also said a self-originated white letter "Iü" on the rock was written by him with his finger.

According to legend, once Milarepa, the greatest yogi of Kagyudpa School of Tibetan Buddhist, was circumambulating the holy mountain clockwise, and again he met Naro Bonchung, the Bon religious master, who was circumambulating Mount

Kailash anti-clockwise. Eventually, when they met again on the huge rock to the northeast valley of the Mount Kailash, they wanted to decide as to which way one should follow on the ritual route. Naro Bonchung again insisted on holding yet another supernatural mystical power competition. A tug of war was held between the two masters, which resulted in the mountain in an anti-clockwise direction. Since then, it is a customary practice of the Bon faith to take an anti-clockwise direction when they circumambulate the holy places including monasteries. Milarepa continued his circumambulation clockwise. As a result, circumambulating clockwise has become the established practice of Buddhist followers. This story explains the origin of the different methods of circumambulating between the Buddhist and Bonpos.

Milarepa and Naro Bonchung both had supernatural powers. Eventually, when they met again on the huge rock in the valley north-east of Mount Kailash, they wanted to decide as to which way one should follow on the ritual route.

Again, Milarepa and Naro Bonchung held a boulder contest. Naro Bonchung piled a yak size stone on a huge boulder. At the mountain, Milarepa piled another stone much bigger than the one Naro Bonchung had piled. Milarepa again matched him by doing exactly the same thing. However, when Milarepa piled up the third stone, Naro could not match him and gave up the spiritual magic contest. Milarepa won the contest over Naro Bonchung. The holy mountain was, thus, owned by Milarepa. This pile of stones is normally called Milarepa and Naro Bonchung's Contest Place. From here, one can see the mountain palace of Snowlion-faced Sky-Walker (སེང་གེ་གདོང་ཅན་) elegantly standing opposite.

When one arrives at a place called Judging of Accumulation of Karmic Merits, one can find a round stone called Melong of Karma. In this place, people have experienced different visions, and those people who are afraid of seeing their merits or demerits, don't pass through the narrow passage between the two stone boulders because it is possible to judge their sins and virtues here.

Anyone who could pass through this passage easily is considered as sinless or less sinful. Any people who are not able to pass through this passage are considered as sinful. It is said that once a great religious Guru was passing through this area with one very sinful man. The Guru went through the passage easily while the sinful man became trapped, unable to pass through, as if something pierced his heart. So this sinful person fervently requested to the religious Guru to get him through this passage and save his life. The religious Guru told him that he should sincerely and whole-heartedly make prayers to his gods, goddesses and they also prayed for his life. The Guru with a chisel and hammer hit at the stone. All of a sudden, blood oozed out of the stone, and the man was freed. This blood is called sinful blood (སྡིག་ཁྲག). One can see the color of blood on the stone even to this day.

A little further from here, there is a passage popularly known as the intermediate passage between death and rebirth (བར་དོའི་འཕྲང་ལམ). It is normally believed to be the most difficult way of the hell. A little further from here, where has to climb up the high mountain on the east side, there is a passage known as Road Leading to Heaven (ལྷ་ལམ་དྲང་ཐག). There is a big stone with self-emanated letter "ཨ" at this mountain, and it is called "Repayment of our Gratitude to Parents". At this particular place, people normally say prayers for their parents. Those who are parentless pray for their departed souls, and those whose parents are alive, pray for their well-being. Near to this place, there is a small spring running down, and it is said that in this water, a courageous Shenpa known as the Butcher of Ling Gesar washed his sinful hands. One can see a handprint of the butcher here, a powerful minister of Ling. Above this place is Dolma La or Dolma pass, also called the Palace of Tara Devi.

There is a short story to tell about Dolma La and why it is called by this name. The height of this famous pass on the ritual circuit of Mount Kailash is 18,200 feet (5500m) above sea level and is the highest point on the outer circuit of pilgrimage. It was necessary to eat some food on this pass, and equally important to share the food with other people even if they were strangers to you. It is also auspicious to hoist prayer flags on the top of this pass. We also consider it beneficial to leave some personal belongings in between the chasms of huge rock on Dolma La. People placed butter offerings on this rock and locks of their hair, some even leave their teeth.

When I was on my pilgrimage and reached this point, the high pass was amazingly impressive. I and my sister and others prostrated three times before the huge rock, as we believed that Tara Devi was present in this rock. We exchanged our foods with others. This exchange of food is considered very auspicious, as we were all together at the holy mountain. The memories of being at the holy pass such as sharing smiles with each other and circumambulating the mountain will keep lingering throughout my life, and peace and harmony will be maintained forever. Thereafter, peace will prevail on the earth, as we believe. When we arrived at Dolma La, there were about 25 to 30 people. Among them, I was the youngest and naughtiest one. Choying, my uncle, and one of the ladies from another place started to perform religious rites with religious instruments like hand drums and kang-ling (rKang-gling) on the edge of Lake Gauri Kund. I, with a very new, recently purchased Tibetan kettle, ran down to Gauri Kund to fetch water for the people waiting on the pass. Pilgrims drink water from this lake because they consider it as nectar (བདུད་རྩི།) and they also take water as a present to their families at home and to other relatives. They also wash their hands and faces. This lake is situated about 100 feet (33 metres) below Tso Kapali. Gauri Kund is 1,320 feet (440 metres) in circumference and it is said that the key to Mount Kailash is in this lake and that of Manasarovara in Lanchen Phug. The lake is situated on the eastern side of Mount Kailash. This small beautiful oval-shaped lake is about three to four miles (five to six and half kilometres) long and half mile (800 metres) wide. Finally, I plucked a few of my hairs and left them in the chasm of Dolma's rock.

No Tibetans have ever heard of or seen this lake completely ice-free. But author Swami Pranavananda has mentioned in his book that, in 1946 and 1947, its ice completely melted away and the author had the unique opportunity of launching his rubber boat Janma Bhoomi on it on 28th August, 1946. He sank his measuring lead into it for the first time and took 51 soundings and the maximum depth recorded was 84 feet. This is the highest lake (18,400 feet (5600 metres) above sea level) ever visited so far by any explorer or surveyer.

Gotsang Gonpo Dorje was on his way to Mount Kailash to discover the outer route for ordinary people, and was always guided by the deities of Mount Kailash and other deities helping him to discover this outer ring. Gonpo, another diety, led Gyawa Gotsang enabling him to circumambulate the route upto Dolma La.

While he was on his ritual circle, he lost his route and prayed to his deities to guide him and show him the way so that future ordinary human beings could go around Mount Kailash. He stood there for a while and meditated on the deities. In deep meditation and prayer, he visualised himself on the perfect path leading to the sacred circle of the path of the Goddess (མཁའ་འགྲོ།). After due prayers he opened his eyes, and found twenty-one green wolves standing in front of him. Since Gotsang Gonpo Dorjee was all by himself and there was no one who could help him in this virgin land. He was frightened by seeing these wolves. But he thought that these animals might have come in a disguise, and he presumed that his deities might have sent these wolves to help him to follow a route to open the road for the ordinary people. So, he slowly walked towards the wolves. The wolves got up and went ahead of him like pet dogs go ahead of their owner. He easily followed them. On reaching the top of the pass, the wolves started disappearing one by one into a rock atop the pass on the back of the Mount Kailash. He realized that Green Tara had come there in the form of wolves. He went straight to the rock and saw the prints of the wolves' feet near the rock and a self-evolved statue of Avalokiteshvara on the rock where he had seen the wolves disappear. Gotsang Gonpo Dorje realized that twenty-one Green Taras had disguised themselves as the wolves to show him the route. Since then, this high pass on the way the ritual circuit around the outer Kailash is called Dolma La. It has also a self-evolved statue of Milarepa visible on the stone, and also an imprinted statue of Milarepa on the rocks of the pass.

Just before reaching the mountain of Tara's Palace, there is also a footprint in the stone left by Drubtob Yongdul who was Drugpa Kagyud. Gyawa Nyonlha's footprint left on the stone has been moved to Zutrulphuk Monastery as a holy object for veneration. The magnificent Elegant Mountain at the west of this place is known as the palace of King Norsang and his Queen Yidrok Lhamo. The majestic mountain at the right side of the pass is Jangchup Chorten. From here, one can see Gonpo Norchen Gangba Sangpo's fort and other lofty mountains too.

One will come across a giant rock on the mountain path at the back of Dolma La where there is footprint of Lama Soepa of the Bon religion, besides the holy lake Khrukyi Zingpo or Purifying Lake at the back of Dolma La. The Indians call it the Gauri Kunda, and it is the bathing pool of Uma or Gauri, the consort of Shiva. The steep road down from this pass is called King with Horse Head (རྟ་མགོ་ཅན།).

A traditional story has it that this lake remains under lid through out the year, and and it is on almost the same altitude as the pilgrimage's trekking circuit. It is also said that the level of water of this lake indicates the fortunes of the people, the yield of harvest, birth of young animals, welfare and security of the country and so forth. In the year of 1940, a big flood occurred from this lake and the level dropped. The water came out from underneath the Ngensong Kundul Tranglam or circuit route. The local people said that the water leaked from the bottom of the holy vase, as they consider it as a vase with pure water. At that time, people could see weapons at the bottom of the lake that had been thrown into this holy lake after the people had renounced killing. So, people considered that the decrease in water level and flood might be bad omens for the whole of the Tibet and Ngari in particular. Exactly in the same year, about 800 strong families of Kyrghiz- Kazakhi and approximately 3000 nomads marched through Ngari in western Tibet, looting, destroying and plundering as they went. These plunderers had left their original homeland in Soviet Central Asia around 1938. For almost three years, they traversed in the Chinese territory of Sinkiang and Qinghai before crossing the Kunlun Mountains and entering Byang thang, the barren northern province of Tibet. Chinese tribes living at the border with Tibet's Qinghai entered the Hor Yerkhen and Hor Yither area. This large group stayed there for almost a year and in the following year, they entered Western Tibet. They terrified almost the whole region of Ngari. Monasteries and people like farmers and nomads along the way were looted, robbed and plundered. Exactly ten years after the unusual flood from the lake, on 28 November 1950, General Lithisen of the Red Chinese Army No. 18, acting on the command of Chinese authorities, led 150 strong well equipped calvalry who invaded the Ngari region from the western side of Kunlun ranges and slowly but steadily occupied Tibet.

The water level of the lake could not regain to its original height, and it remained a small lake over the years. But now the level of this lake is increasing, and it is considered a sign of good luck for the people of Tibet.

Just below the trekking route, one can see a footprint of the Seventh Reincarnated Lama Kagyud Thinley Shingta. This foot print is very clear. Because it is on the side of the road, it is easy to see while on the ritual trek. At the right side of this rocky mountain, there are idols of deities like Sky-Walker Lion-faced

One, Vajrapani, and Tamdin or Hayagriva. Today, this place is called Lekitare and is said to be the head of deity Hyagriva. When one walks a little down from Lekitare, one will arrive at a place called Melongteng (Above Mirror). Here is a set of self-originated footprints of horse, said to be the footprints of great King Ling Gesar's horse.

Near to this, on the rock, there are a few other footprints believed to be of the great saint Milarepa from when he was circumambulating Mount Kailash and met with Bon Master Naro Bonchung circumambulating from the opposite direction. Milarepa tried to take Naro Bonchung with him on the clockwise circumambulation of the Mount Kailash. It has become the usual practice that Buddhists go clockwise and Bonpos go anti-clockwise when circumambulating holy stupas, lakes and other holy sites. A little down from there on the right side of river bank, there are three to four footprints which are said to be the footprints left by the great saints Milarepa and Naro Bonchung.

To the left, one can see a typical mountain landscape of sharp, weapon-like summits. These peaks are called the palace of Lhamo Yitrokma. The soaring mountain on the right side is called the Abode of Deity Palgon Dhonchu or Shalmariye mythical tree, a tree of hell, the leaves of which are sharp-pointed resembling swords.

Just above the foothill of this pass, there is a rock ball and its top is known as Northeast Immutable (བྱང་ཤར་མི་འགྱུར་བའི་གཟེར།) on which Shabje Dragtok (rock with footprints of Lord Buddha) is visible. This is the northeast immutable sacred nailing of Mount Kailash. At a little distance from the green meadow near the mountain there is a spot blessed with footprints of Padmasambhava on a small white-stone passage known as Big Lion Stone Bridge (སེང་ཆེན་རྫ་ཟམ།). Below this place, there is a footprint of 'Dro-mgon gTsang-pa rGya-ras (Dogon Tsangpa Gyare), the great yogic practitioner, who had spent years on Mount Kailash. To the east of this area, there is a self-originated image of Wrathful Bodhisattva Deity (ཁྲོ་བོ་མི་གཡོ་བ་-) and Mahadeva (མགོན་པོ།). The great yogic practitioner Drugchen Tsangpa Gyare saw these deities, who vanished into the rock leaving behind the imprints on the rock. There is also an imprint of the deity Dorje Phagmo as seen by Gyawa Nyonglha. To the east of mKha'-'dro'i Sanglam or Sky-Walker's Secret Route, which we consider the eastern gate of the Mount Kailash known as Chagtsalkhang, is where people pray with folded hands and their heads bowed down. At the lower corner of mKha'-'dro Sanglam mountain, there is another mountain known as Deity Tashi Tseringma's abode. On the eastern bank of Zongchu River, there is a footprint of Drukchen Tsangpa Gyare.

A little farther from the footprint of Drukchen Tsangpa Gyare and at a corner, there is a mountain known as *Sangs rgyas sman lha'i pho brang* (སངས་རྒྱས་སྨན་ལྷའི་ཕོ་བྲང་) which resembles a golden house, wherein there are different kinds of medicinal herbs and desease-curing springs, hence it is regarded as the place of Medicine Buddha. In the neck of this mountain are the caves of Drigung Yogis; its beauty attracts visitors. It is said that there are about 180 caves on Mount Kailash.

Near the Zongchu River, there is a huge stone with five colors which is known as Medicine Buddha's Medicine Grinding Stone. A small tent-size stone is there which is known as the Medicinal Bag of Medicine Buddha. There are two lofty mountain ranges on the right side of the palace of Medicine Buddha, and near Tashi Tseringma's place, known as the place of Namthose, and Tashi Gomang stupa "རྣམ་ཐོས་སྲས་དང་བཀྲིས་སྒོ་མང་མཆོད་རྟེན།"

A few steps beyond the stupa of Tashi Gomang, on the upper side of the road, there is a footprint of Tsangnyon Heruka on a stone. At the lower side of this road, to the left of Menlhas's fort of Medicine Buddha, there is a mountain exactly shaped like a garuda. Because of its shape, it is called Yeshi Khyung palace. It is located on the southern side of Mount Menlha. In that mountain, Shri Guhyasamaja (དཔལ་གསང་བ་འདུས་པ) and the deity Black Dzambala's palace (ཇམ་སེར་ནག་གི་ཕོ་བྲང་།) A mountain range shaped as a stupa is popularly known as eight *bDe gshegs* (བདེ་གཤེགས་མཆོད་རྟེན) and there is a self-originated image of deity Vajrayogini (Dorje Phagmo) whom the rocks resemble.

Adjacent to the Menlha abode, there is a holy hat print of Gyawa Karmapa in the stone. On the side of rock-hill and behind of Zutrulphuk Monastery, there is a unique lofty mountain known as the Abode of the Kailash Protector Deities. It is said that Drubtob Guru Tsechen invited Milarepa to his cave while the great saint was spending his time at Mount Kailash. The great Milarepa inscribed the a letter "A" with his finger in the rock and since then, it is called Aa-Phug or Cave of Letter "ཨ".

According to legend, Zutrulphuk monastery was erected in memory of another contest held between Milarepa and Naro Bonchung.

Once Milarepa and Naro Bonchung met at this particular place, when weather was not good, and both were proceeding to circumambulate the Mount Kailash. (Milarepa was proceeding clockwise and Naro Bonchung anti-clock wise.) Both of them found a safe, dry place to have shelter, as it was raining. It was agreed between them to construct a small stone building as a shelter from rain that had already soaked their clothes. The Great Milarepa asked Naro Bonchung whether he would build walls or put a roof on the building. Naro Bonchung replied that he wished to build the four walls, and by magic, he collected enough in a short time. Milarepa looked at him with envy, but the stones were heavy for Naro Bonchung to pick up to build the walls. He looked with dispirited eyes at Milarepa, and then Milarepa released his magical power, and thus built the four walls. Milarepa had broken a huge slab of stone to protect them against rain, but the entire roof of stone building was installed by Naro Bonchung. After they had built this small shelter, when both of them were entering inside the small room they had built, as its height was little low, Milarepa lifted the roof with his head and hand, leaving an imprint of his head and hand on the stone roof. When he saw it to be lifted for them, Milarepa climbed upon the roof and stamped it down with his feet and footprints appeared on top of the roof. These imprints of Great Master Milarepa still exist on the stone rooftop at the cave by Zultrulphuk Monastery.

As Milarepa and Naro Bonchung had jointly built this small stone house with their magical power, it came to be known as Magic Cave. Later on, a monastery was built over there by the followers of Kagyudpa and was called Zultrulphuk Monastery (རྫུ་འཕྲུལ་ཕུག་དགོན་པ།) (Magic Cave monastery). Those stones used for the walls were the ones which Naro could not lift up. They are the bigger stones which were too heavy to be lifted by Naro Bonchung because Milarepa had used his magical powers to make those stones heavy; many such stones were left at the site. There are also small stones that were broken at the time of magical contest. It is an interesting point for the research scholars to study and research. The legendary religious contest was held in late 11th century between the two most powerful religious figures in the Kagyud and Bon religions. The best-known small stone structured Drubphug was built during the spread of Buddhism (བསྟན་པ་ཕྱི་དར།) in Guge Kingdom during its glory period.

From its establishment until 1960, there had been continuous flow of great meditators, retreatants and scholars of Kagyudpa who lived and spent their lives in this monastery. During the Chinese Cultural Revolution, forced upon the Tibetans under the Chinese occupation, this monastery was destroyed and demolished. The main statues in this monastery were a golden statue of Milarepa, an alloyed metal Buddha's statue, gold images of Guru Nangsi Zilnon, Kyopa Jigten Gon, and Bhutanese Lama Ngawang Namgyal. The Drukpa Kagyud School financed and managed this monastery. Lord Buddha's holy white footprint is located nearby this monastery on the eastern side of Mount Kailash. This is the eastern immutable sacred nailing of Mount Kailash. Below this area, there is a spring called Damze Kedun's (Seven-Birth Brahmin) holy water. Long ago, Drubtob Kunga Sangpo was on his way to circumambulate Mount Kailash, he was on the ridge of the mountain, having passed Zultruphuk Monastery, when he had a glimpse of deity Vajrayogini (Dorje Phagmo) on the other side of Zonchu River at the mountain. He at once prayed to the deity and the deity left her footprint on the stone.

Below this holy place, on the mani ground (མ་ཎི་གདང་), there is clear footprint of Sakya Gongma Rinpoche on a beautiful mandala area. At the corner of Gedhen Lhachu, there is a footprint of Lhayak Tolpo Karpo. A little further above this point, there is a place called Broken Stone (ཕ་བོང་གས་པོ་) Gangri Karchag said that one day Kalon Denma of Ling Gesar was on his way to ritually circumambulate Mount Kailash when he met his enemy Dulon Bitra Ngamdul. As enemies, they wanted to kill each other. So, a fierce battle started between them. When Dulon Bitra Ngamdul took out his heavy sword and tried to hit Kalon Denma to chop his whole body into two pieces, but he could not be hit, as the sword was too heavy. He hit it on a big stone. The stone was broken into two pieces. Kalon Denma took out his bow and shot an arrow at Dulon Bitra. The arrow pierced through the heart of his enemy, and he was killed then and there killed. The stone broken by the sword is known as Phabong Gepo or Broken Stone.

If one goes little further, one will come across a beautiful place called the Dancing Place of the Sky-Walkers (མཁའ་འགྲོའི་བྲོ་ར་), the protector-deities of Mount Kailash. The few footprints visible on the rock are said to be formed by Sky-Walkers while they were dancing. Not very far away, there stands a big elegant stone which is said to be the holy flesh of the Seven-Birth Brahmin (བྲམ་ཟེ་སྐྱེ་བདུན་ཤ་ཁ།).

A little below from here, there is a narrow passage called Yellow and Red Road. There is a footprint of Chenga

Drigunglingpa on the upper part of the passage, along with a footprint of Kalon Denma and his horse. The footprints of a man and a dog are on the rock too. I was told that these were the prints of the great hunter Gonpo Dorje and his hunting dog. On the roadside to Mount Kailash, there is an imprint of entire body of a lady dressed completely drong (yak) and also an imprint of a devil drong (yak) that was subdued by King Gesar Gyalpo. It is considered to be the yak of demon-king Achung Gyalpo. It is interesting to see all these imprints on rocks and their related legends.

After reaching a beautiful place called rZong-lung, as described by Drubchen Lingre, one can feel like,

རྫོང་ལུང་མཐུན་རྐྱེན་འཛོམས་པོ་དེ། །
དགོས་འདོད་ཐམས་ཅད་འབྱུང་བའི་རྟགས། །

"rZong-lung has everything (in abundance),
It is a sign of fulfillment of all the wishes."
(as all medicinal herbs are available there).

This holy place has various kinds of stones, soil, water, herbs, trees and grass. All these are considered to have the holy properties that can fulfil our wishes and desires, and some of them can cure diseases and protect us from evil spirits too. This place is known as the Door of Treasure Store (འདོད་རྒུ་དཔག་མེད་ འབྱུང་བའི་འཛོམས་མདོའི་སྒོ) and the Eastern Gate, one of the four gates of Mount Kailash. In between Dharchen and Dharchung, there is a sand mountain called Jaklungphuri, which looks like a woman's breast and is said to be breast of demoness (ལྷག་ལུང་ཕུ་ རི་སྲིན་མོའི་ནུ་མ). In between these two sand hills, there is a cave popularly known to be a leprosy healing vajra cave which is blessed and purified by Lord Avalokiteshvara.

If one climbs up from the Dharchen trading centre there is a mountain called Downward Creeping Poisonous Snake (དུག་སྦྲུལ་ ཐུར་རྒྱགས) on which majestic Gyangtak Monastery is situated.

This monastery is one of the oldest monasteries around Mount Kailash and Lake Manasarovara. Dharchen is a place where different sects and religions gather. In ancient times, the folks from the Indian foothills, the nomads from distant provinces of Tibet, the rich merchants from Lhasa, ascetics, brigands, Bonpos, Hindus and Buddhists mingled here with spiritual fervour and and in order to intensify their purification and accumulate merits through their religious activities. Still today faith and devotion has brought them together and unites them within a single spirit that has transcended all divergences and controversies. When you reach here, you see the power of faith in their eyes; obviously they have forgotten hardship they faced during their long and arduous journey. They chant, prostrate, and circumambulate together until they disperse late at night to sleep. All of them seem to have a good guide: one who is not there does not mean to show them the geographical route like the one or modern, but one conversant with the uncharted depth of inner space. Everyone will feel here that God is with them. One realizes that the spiritual world for him is as real as the material world is for other people. The faithful devotees will forget the materialistic world, and they engage themselves in pursuing spiritual goals. The ascetics would equally pity those who take their chance for bliss that can only be attained by following the spiritual life instead of the vain pursuit of desires.

The great saint Guhaya Gangpa spent 25 years on Mount Kailash meditating and preaching religion to his faithful disciples. It is said that one day, when Guhaya Gangpa was meditating in the cave, a group of seven Indian sadhus came to offer him an amount of gold the size of deer head which he refused to accept. (ཉིན་གཅིག་ཏེ་སེ་ཞིང་སྟོང་གིས་རྒྱ་གར་གྱི་རྟ་གི་བདུན་དུ་སྤྲུལ་ནས་བདུན་ཡོང་ཏེ་ཕྱག་བྱས་ནས། གསེར་ཤ་བའི་མགོ་ཚད་ཞིག་ཕུལ་བྱུང་།) He was purely a religious man who had already denounced worldly pleasure and attachment. (རྟར་འཛིན་པས། བྱ་བ་བཏང་བའི་གནས་རྣལ་འབྱོར་ལ་རིན་ཆེན་གསེར་གྱི་དགོས་པ་མེད། གསུངས་ནས་མ་བཞེས་པས།) At that very moment, his teacher Kyobpa Jigten Sumgon appeared in

the sky riding on a white lion and commanded his disciple
Guhaya Gangpa to accept the gold offered to him by saying,

> "Saintly son! Give up hesitation,
> Protecting deity has offered gift,
> Take for good omen,
> Place prophesied by Buddha in the neck of Tise.
>
> Valley faced in eastern county,
> There is a mountain like an elephant standing
> Showing his trunk in the upland,
> And the lower end of county is in like Mudra posture,
> The backside is as if it covered with white curtain,
> The sky blue is of eight-spoked auspicious wheel,
> The land is shaped like eight-petalled) lotus,
> In jostling of rock and water, eight lucky symbols brighten,
> Meeting of Rock hill and grassland symbolizes seven Royal
>   jewels.
>
> In front of good shaped mountain appears a tent put up,
> On the back of creeping down black snake,
> White rock like a big tent put up and on the top,
> To sound oneness (shunyata) of phenomenon.
> May be decorated by clear "ཨ "
> In the place of assembling Mother Sky-Walkers like clouds,
> Build a renowned monastery,
> It will benefit whole Tibet in general and
> In particular, the Kagyud tradition will be blossomed
>   forth."

The monastery was built as commanded but under Red Chinese
occupation and rule, this ancient and unique monastery was
also destroyed. While destroying the monastery, many precious
religious books and priceless idols, and thangkas were also
destroyed. However in 1986, this monastery was rebuilt by
Lama Wangthang Dorjee. Now, pilgrims can visit the monastery.

Three hundred meters above the Gyangtak Monastery, there are stone buildings. According to our old Zhangzhung record, these old ruins of buildings belonged to the Zhangzhung Dynasty and were built by a Zhangzhung king at the time of Bon Tonpa Shenrab and are where Tonpa Shenrab preached his first sermon of Bon. Lovers of archaeology and culture and humanities can research at the site now and for the benefit of the future.

The holy idol in this monastery is Buddha Langdul Chunyerma (ཕྱུབ་དབང་གླང་འདུལ་ཆུ་གཉེར་མ།). The written and oral tradition recorded by past generations describe how the monastery received this holy statue. Based on the religious texts, I want to write a brief account of how the monastery procured the most holy statue from Gonpo Ben that was made during the time of Lord Buddha. One day, during the time of Lord Buddha, King Bimbisara (གཟུགས་ཅན་སྙིང་པོ།) of Magadha in India, the king of God Gyajin, and the king of Naga Gawo had a meeting and discussed works to be carried out, if Lord Buddha passed away or attained Mahaparinirvana. In order to pay due respect to him, to remember his good deeds and for prayers, they considered idols of him were needed for future generations. So, the three kings unanimously agreed to make a humble request to Lord Buddha to create and leave his idol for the future. Lord Buddha told them to bring their precious materials so that he could prepare idols for to satisfaction.

Accordingly, the three kings brought their copper basins full of precious stones and jewels, and put them in front of Lord Buddha. He told them that they should come and collect their idols after seven days. Lord Buddha miraculously made his own image as per the number of the precious stones.

The king of God Gyajin received an idol of Buddha measuring twelve feet (4 metres), the king of Naga Gawo got an idol of Buddha six feet (2 metres) in height and; the king Bimbisara of Magadha got a Lord Buddha idol just twelve inches (30 centimetres) in height. They took their idols and happily returned to their own palaces and kept their idols in their respective shrines of their kingdoms. However, Gonpo Ben, a demon, who was living near Mount Kailash and owned the Lakar Lake, took away the idol that belonged to the Magadha king. Later on, when Lord Buddha and his 500 disciples visited and blessed Mount Kailash, the Buddha instructed Gonpo Ben and the Naga king of Lake Mapham to keep this holy idol until the Five-Hundred Arhats of his followers paid a visit to this holy lake. At that time, they should hand over the idol to his followers who were visiting Mount Kailash and Lake Manasarovara to encourage Buddhism in the region for the benefit of human beings. As a consequence, Kagyudpas sent successive but huge number of meditators, saints, religious reformers and yogic practitioners to Mount Kailash, Manasarovara and other parts of Ngari. It is said that in those days like the twinkling of stars in the sky, many great practitioners of Kagyudpas had spent their lives in the mountains of Ngari.

During the peak time of flourishing of Kagyudpa teaching in western Tibet, a great saint by the name of Drigung Lingpa alias Chennga Sherab Jungney was spending time at Mount Kailash and Manasarovara Lake. He was invited to visit the king of Naga at Lake Manasarovara and offered the idol of Thubwang Langdul Chunyerma. He took it to Gyangtak Monastery, and it became the holiest idol in the monastery and remained there until the year 1959. The religious affiliation of this well-known monastery is Drigung Kagyud. Drigung Kyabgon Rinpoche appoints the head lama of this monastery.

In 1959, during the Tibetan National Uprising against the forceful occupation of Tibet by the Chinese and subsequent killings of unarmed Tibetans by the Chinese military force, one of the monks from the monastery kept the idol, and it is safe and sound there. The footprints of Drigung Lingpa Chennga Chokyi Gyalpo and Drigung Chokyi Lodoe are also at this monastery. In front of the Mount Kailash to the east side of the monastery is situated Guhaya) Gangpa's Retreat Place. Anyone wishing to study more about the monastery can read the book titled *Karchak Ngulkar Melong of the Mount Kailash,* written by Drigung Chungtsang Rinpoche in 1896 AD, while he was living at Kakshung on the Ladakh-Tibet border. He based the text on the early Gangri Karchak written by the Third Shamar Rinpoche. This book is not only important to study about Mount Kailash and Lake Manasarovara but also it is very important to learn the history of Ngari. Another nearby holy place to visit is the place of footprints of Lord Buddha and his 500 disciples known as the South Immutable Sacred Nail of Mount Kailash, also known as Shabje Thongdol. We believe that one who looks at those footprints will gain sufficient spiritual merits to do away with their entire demerits and ignorance forever.

If one proceeds eastward, there is a place called Metokting where there is a cave and a small spring. It is known as Drigung Drubtob Nagpo's cave, and utilizes water from this spring. From the place called Shabje Draktog (Footprint Rock) on the upper part of the hill, there is a hill resembling a throne that it is known as Throne of Lord Buddha from which he preached Lhubum (Klu-'bum) to Lu Mado (Klu Ma-dros), the serpent king Lu Tsugna Rinchen (Klu gTsugna Rinchen) of Manasarovara Lake. We still call it "Lord Buddha's Throne" and Tise Lo rGyus says that Lord Buddha sat on this rock and preached teachings to God (ལྷ།), Naga (Klu, ཀླུ།) and human beings (མི།); the sutra preached is known as Lankavatara Sutra (ལང་ཀར་གཤེགས་པའི་མདོ།).

At the base of Mount Poe-ri Ngadan (རི་སྤོས་རི་དང་ལྡན།, sPos ri Ngad ldan) or Fragrant Incense Mountain and during the middle period of the Zhangzhung dynasty in Upper Tibet, there were eighteen powerful horn-bearing kings. During this time the Bon Tonpa Shenrab, Triwer Laje Sergyi Jaruchen (Khri Wer La rje Gulang gSergyi Byaruchan), the holder of golden horn of the bird was living at this place. He built Se Khang

Norbu Tsekpa (གསས་ཁང་ནོར་བུ་བརྩེགས་པ།, Gsas Khang Norbu brTsegs-pa), a Bon temple, as its auspicious location. Tonpa Shenrab gave divine blessings to all living beings including to this great king of Zhangzhung. He received direct religious teachings from Tonpa Shenrab and a text called Do Lungten (mDo Lung-bsten). The same text can be found in our Sungdu (gSung bsdus) and the scripts are the same as we find in a collection of Bon sutras (མཆོ་མང་།).

While visiting Gyangtak Monastery, one can see old Zhangzhung period stone built ruins scattered above the monastery. Bellezza writes that these buildings, located above the Gyangtak Monastery, are at an elevation of 5400 meters above sea level. Gyangtak itself is located at 5100 meters and below the old ruined buildings (རྫ་ཁང་།). We normally say that Gyangtak is one of the highest monasteries in Tibet. But the Zhang Zhung stone building (རྫ་ཁང་།) is situated 300 meters higher than the Gyangtak Monastery. This indicates either that the native people lived at such a high altitude or its mountain grew higher in recent times.

The stone buildings were actually located at Darlung valley, above the Dharchen trade centre of Tise Barkha Tazam. Bellezza (2001, p. 62) writes:

"In the inner circuit (Nang skor) of Gangs bkar Tise, located, primary above the Drigungpa monastery of Gyangtak (rGyang rgrags), are the carcasses of more than 30 of building all-stones structures. The presence of so many ancient edifices attests to the long-lived religious and cultural importance of Gangs Tise. Locally called stone house, the identity of these ancient structures largely escaped local attention, nor does it seem to be directly addressed in the sacred geographic gnas bshad and bkar chag literature hof Gangs Tise. According to local sources, these structures were used by meditators of yore, which given their lofty aspect and location, is very plausible. There are important knt factors that seem to indicate that at least a portion of the stone houses were founded in the pre-Buddhist period, (1) the prominent position of Gyangtak (rGyang rgrags) in Zhang Zhung history. (2) The all stone construction and other archaic design features of the rdo khang. (3) Their extremely altitudinous aspect. (4) their neglect in the Buddhist oral and textual history of Gang Tise".

Below this point and near to the snow-capped range, there is a cave with a spring that was once used by the great yogi Drigung Lingpa. During the time of Drigung Lingpa, there were many yogic practitioners who spent their lives on Mount Kailash. We can see so many caves all around this area. To the west of Gyangtak Monastery, there is a pass called Lhadar Gang. At the back of this pass, there is a valley called Se-lung. Drubtob Buchung of the Drigung Kagyud school founded a small shrine of deities and established a temple and retreat center for the meditators, yogic practitioners and followers of his school. During the evil days of the iron-fisted forceful Chinese occupation this temple, shrine and retreat center were not spared but were completely destroyed by Chinese Red Guards under their Cultural Revolution.

Fortunately in 1987, Lama Wangthang Dorje has rebuilt this temple and the shrine, and a few meditators have re-started tantric yogic practices at this place. Behind Selung, there is a rocky mountain called Sheldrak (Shel-Brag, Glass Rock Mountain). Along the roadside of the inner pilgrimage circuit on the upper part of the rock, there is a self-originated image of the horse-head deity Hayagriva. This Glass Rock Mountain appears in the shape of the SevenPrecious Gems (རྒྱལ་སྲིད་རིན་ཆེན་ སྣ་བདུན།, rGyalsrid sNa-mdon).

If we move to the back of this mountain, we will reach a beautiful valley where we will find a big stone boulder resembling a lama's hat being put on it by a yogic practitioner. Below this stone, there is a cave whose presence was foretold by Drigung Kyobpa, known as Prophesied Cave (ལུང་བསྟན་ཕུག).

At the front and below the Glass Rock Mountain, there are many caves used by the great yogic practitioners including Drubchen Singe Yeshi. On the top of Glass Rock Mountain is a palace of Lord Shiva. Besides the rocky mountain, there is the small hillock called Monkey Holding Incense, as described earlier. Just below this mountain, there is a hillock that resembles a frog. The great Drubchen Singe Yeshi had keys to open this holy cave where thirteen golden stupas were built later. We can see here the imprints of a key (སྒོ་ལྡེ་མིག) and a crow on the stone. From Glass Rock Mountain, along the inner pilgrimage circuit of Mount Kailash one can come across a wonderful rocky valley resembling a vajra which surrounds the area.

In this a high mountainous area, Lama Tsultrim Gonpo did enormous work spreading the teachings of Drigung Kagyud, and he built his followers' confidence about the great teachings of his master. He also worked hard to maintain the teachings promote and sustain religious activities for our future life. He built a golden stupa in memory of his great teacher Chenga Lingpa, the second in the line of Drigung Kagyud Lamas. During the reign of King Tashi Ngodup of the Yatse dynasty of Ngari that the Ngari became faithful followers of Drigung teachers. The Yatse royal families made large financial contributions to Lama Tsultrim Gonpo to help him build the huge golden statue of his master.

In comparision to other neighboring small principalities, the Yatse dynasty was quite rich in almost all fields. This dynasty promised to provide full support to the Drigung Kagyud especially the Dharma practitioners at the Mount Kailash (called in Tibetan རིས་པ). They supplied necessaries for practice at Mount Kailash including warm clothes, and food, and arranged the due facilities essential for the ripas. Thus the ripas had no material problems and things were made available and easy for them to stay at the mountain to attain enlightenment and improve their lives. The Yatse also made promises to supply finance as well as future food and clothes for the practitioners of Drigung at Mount Kailash, Lake Manasarovara and its surrounding areas.

At one time, five hundred yogis lived in "bird shelters" on Kailash where they attained special merits. Drigung Tise Lorgyus says that Dozin (rDo-'dzin) Darma Gyaltsen arrived at the Mount Kailash around 1278.

Until the time of Abbot Tsultrim Gonpo when the Chos kyi rgyalpo was the abbot at Drigung (1351-1407), the ripas at Mount Kailash were fully patronized by the kings of Yatse and Khunnu; all were the staunch followers of Drigung Kagyud.

Drigung's Tise text (page 32a lines 3-6) states;

དེ་ནས་བཟུང་གདན་རབས་བཅུ་གཅིག་པ་འཛམ་གླིང་ཆོས་ཀྱི་རྒྱལ་པོའི་སློབ་
མ་རྡོར་འཛིན་ཚུལ་ཁྲིམས་མགོན་པོ་བར་ལུང་སྟོགས་ཀྱི་ཡོན་ཏན་ཕུན་སུམ་
ཚོགས་པ་མངའ་བའི་རྡོར་འཛིན་པ་མུ་ཏིག་བསྟར་ལ་བརྒྱུས་པ་བཞིན་བྱོན་
ཞིང་། རིས་པ་ཡང་ཉུང་མཐར་ལྔ་བརྒྱ་ལས་མ་ཉུང་བ་བྱུང་བའི་སྦྱིན་བདག་ནི་
མངའ་རིས་སྐོར་གསུམ་ཁུ་ནུ་བཅས་ཀྱི་རྒྱལ་བློན་རྣམས་དང་ཡང་ཡ་རྩེ་
ཡང་འཛམ་གླིང་ཆོས་ཀྱི་རྒྱལ་པོ་རིམ་ཕེབས་རྣམས་ཀྱིས་མཛད་ནས་རྟེན་
གསུམ་བཞེངས་པ་དང་། དགེ་འདུན་རི་ཁྲོད་པ་རྣམས་ལ་འཚོ་རྟེན་གྱ་ནོམ་པ་
སྦྱར་བ་དང་། མཐའ་དམག་གི་འཇིགས་པ་སྲུང་བ་སོགས་མཛད།

de nas bzung gdan rab bcu gcig pa 'dzam gling chos kyi rgyalpo'i slob-ma rdor-'dzin Tsultrim mgonpoi bar lung stogs kyi yon tan phun-gsum tshogs pa mnga-bai rdor-dzin pa mutig bstarla brgyus pa bzhin byon zhing! Ris-pa yang nyung mthar lnga brgya las ma-nyungba byung bai sbyin bdag ni mNga'-ris skor-gsum khunnu bcas kyi rgyal blon rnam dang yang ya-rtse Dzumlang 'dzam-gling chos kyi rgyalpo rimphebs rnams kyi mdzad nas rten gsum bzhengs pa dang! dGe dun ri-khrod pa rnams la 'tsho rten gya nompa sbyarba dang! mTha dmag gi 'jigspa srungba sogs mdzad.

Abbot Tsultrim Gonpo was a disciple of the Eleventh Drigung abbot Zamling Choekyi Gyalpo (dZam-gling Chos kyi rGyalpo). His disciples addressed him as rDo rje 'dzin-pa, meaning righteous qualities of well-understood teachings that came like a string of pearls.

Abbot Tsultrim Gonpo was a highly learned great scholar of that time. He was spiritualist and a great tantric teacher. He had many royal followers from Ngari that included the Yatse Dynasty. Those royal families gave unflinching moral as well as financial support. It is said that the kings and ministers of Ngari Korsum particularly Khunnu, and the Yatse lineage of Jumla kings of Nepal, were all sincere and staunch followers of its religion who made three kinds of receptacles. The Yatse lineage of Jumla kings took special pleasure in providing sustenance to the monks and the hermits. They strongly believed that monks and hermits were the defenders the country against the threat of border raids and invasion. However, it seems that this situation changed after the tenure of the Eleventh Abbot; it appears that this period fell close to the resurgence of power of Guge during the second half of the 14th century (1363).

Later on, the number of the hermits at Mount Kailash went down from 500 to a few scattered ripas living in caves at Mount Kailash. We don't know the exact reasons for the decrease of Ripas. It is my understanding that reasons discussed below led to the decrease of ripas at Mount Kailash.

Firstly, it was in 1290 that the Prince of Timor Buqa carried out a strong military raid on the Drigung Kagyud along with Sakya Ponchen Aglen Dorje Pal (ས་སྐྱ་དཔོན་ཆེན་ཨག་ལེན་རྡོ་རྗེ་དཔལ།). This raid on Drigung in 1290 was generally called destroying the Foundation of Drigung Kagyu or Drigung gling log (འབྲི་གུང་གླིང་ལོག). It is said that during the invasion and raid on Drigung Monastery, thousands of great Drigung Drubchens flew up into the air. To be frank enough, thousands of great lamas too lost their lives during the raid.

Secondly, when thousands of great Drubchens flew away into the air, there were no more of Drubchens left behind in Tibet who could guide and preach the great spiritual teachings and tantric practices to the young enthusiatic novices.

Thirdly, when the Guge Kingdom finally collapsed in 1633, there were no royal supporters or sponsors for the ripas Mount Kailash due to the change of political administration in Ngari. The number of ripas decreased, although Tibetan Government still collected taxes from the people to be paid to the ripas.

Later on, the Drigung lineage built golden stupas in the same site as the second lineage of their head lama who had passed away at an advanced age. Normally, we call them the Thirteen Golden Stupas (གསེར་གདུང་བཅུ་གསུམ།), but in reality, there were seventeen golden stupas. It was said that thirteen stupas were inside the chamber and the rest could not be accommodated in the Chamber due to the lack of space. During the sad and unfortunate days of the Cultural Revolution, all the golden stupas were destroyed. The Tibetan people in Western Tibet and the followers of Drigung Kagyud have already rebuilt all the golden stupas on the old sites. Without a visit to these stupas, it is considered that a trip to Mount Kailash is incomplete and meaningless, and the holy place itself is completed only after the completion of the thirteen circumambulations of the Mount Kailash. The monuments of Drigung Kagyud abbots were kept at this particular place, making Mount Kailash a holy spot for the pilgrims. The particular place is called Serdung Cho-sum. From here, one can see Barkha Tazam plain and Rakshas Tal with its gallery of mountain peaks, extending to the Indian borders, creating a superb unique landscape. Dharchen is approximately eleven kilometres from here. The distance between the Serdung Cho-sum and Dharchen is not very far, but the whole distance is almost one continuous steep ascent over sharp stone and moraines. The Drigung Kagyud head monastery is situated about 100 (140 kilometres) from Lhasa. The monuments were located on mountainous ranges to save them from frequent destruction caused by notorious avalanches and rock falls. Gyangtak Monastery takes care of these monuments, and they periodically repair the golden statues with paint and gilding.

In front of these golden stupas, there is a mountain that appears as a heap of precious gemstone called Neten Yenlagjung's Palace. The left side of this mountain resembles a loosely hanging white curtain. This hill is called the palace of deity Yeshi Gonpo Lhatsok. These two lakes are situated at the heartlands of the hills, and they are regarded as being sources holy nectar with medicinal herbs. The Gangri Karchag (ri sKar chag) text says,

"mKha' 'dgro gsang ba du pai khrus kyi bdud rtsi dkhyil bai mtso gnyis yod de ..!"

"མཁའ་འགྲོ་གསང་བ་འདུ་བའི་ཁྲུས་ཀྱི་བདུད་རྩི་འཁྱིལ་བའི་མཚོ་གཉིས་ཡོད་ དེ། ཅེས་གསུངས།"

Right below this foothill, one can have a view of the sacred lakes Kapali (or Tso Kapali) and Tulkyi Zingbu. The Hindus call Kapali lake Rakta and in Gangri Karchag (Gangs ri sKar chag), it is said that the water of Rakta is a brown in color, and it is like chang (traditional home-brewed Tibetan beer). The colour of the water of this lake is black or brown due to the black stones at its bed. The circumference of this lake is 660 feet (200 metres) and is situated 100 feet (30 metres) above the Gauri Lake. The lake is located amidst bare stones with no sign of earth as far as the eye could see. Yet at a few places in the bed of the Kapali Lake, a very soft alluvial soil is detected by the pilgrims and they take samples of the soil as a souvenir of the holy places. This holy lake is situated 4.5 miles (6.3 kilometres) from the Serdung Cho-sum and east of Neten Yenlagjung.

Gauri Kund Lake is at an altitude of about 18,200 feet (5547 metres). This holy lake almost perpetually remains frozen throughout the year. Again, local legend explains how the lake came to be frozen all year round. It is said that in ancient time, this lake did not freeze during the summer. The Tibetans also identify this lake as a Tulkyi Zingbu or Nectar Lake (བདུད་རྩི་ མཚོ།) and its looks like milky water. Due to the holiness of the water, people took advantage of the open lake. They went there with their families to wash their sinful hands and hair. One day, however, a baby accidentally slipped into the lake from its mother's hands and drowned. So the guardian deity, in the interest of safety, made the lake to remain perpetually frozen. The mother of the drowned baby was in shock and to remove her sin, at full speed she made thirteen circumambulations of Mount Kailash. After her last circuit, she took a rest and the full imprint of her body became imprinted on the rock where she rested. Since then, we say that anyone who makes at least thirteen circumambulations around the outer circuit, isconsidered properly qualified to make a ritual visit to the lake. As with Tso Kapali, those who visit the lake take samples of soil as holy prasada or souvenirs. Local people say that a drop of holy water fell from the heaven to form the River Ganges, and four other drops are the four rivers that flow in four directions from Mount Kailash. According to Norsang Lhamo Opera, there is a nectar lake or Tulkyi Zingbu where Lhamo Yidrog was purified on the 15th day of a month by a holy hermit known as Kyiburi Drubchen. She was subsequently captured by a "holder of plank" (སྒྱུང་ལེབ་འཛིན་པ་), a fisher man, for his bride but was saved by the hermit and later on was given away to King Norsang as his queen.

So far as my knowledge goes, this is how we end our whole circle of holy pilgrimage of Mount Kailash (parikrama). Any one wishing to make a trip to the holy mountain, as I have mentioned above, should go right around. As a matter of fact, every side of Mount Kailash has a peculiar charm, grace, attraction and beauty of its own. There are so many indescribably fascinating things to see and visit while going round the peak of Mount Kailash. At every hour, the holy mountain will present you with a fresh fantastic scene and, at each turn, reveal new glimpses and beauties of the mountain. Those who have gone to Mount Kailash for a ritual circuit must have learnt how to appreciate and enjoy the beauty of nature and the mountain's grandeur and glory.

The Mount Kailash is the holiest of several holy places (tirtha) in the Himalayas. Whether you are a follower of Buddhism, Bon, Hinduism, Christianity or Islam, or even an atheist, or, whatsoever religion you may belong to, you will definitely be irresistibly, unknowingly and unconsciously drawn to the divine presence, that is the hidden truth behind this apparent vast universe.

We should be grateful to the thousands of our ancestors who explored the most inaccessible mountains, forests and regions in the Himalayas thousands of years ago. They went to every nook and corner of these snow-covered mountains. They held silent communion with nature. These great yogis discovered the best of the mountains' view points and panoramic sceneries. Our great masters enjoyed their comprehensive beauty and bequeathed them as a legacy by way of the places of pilgrimage: from the most inaccessible mountains, streams, rivers, brooks and springs. Passes and places have been stamped with their names which is a proof of this statement. In summary, their very blood, their best writings, both spiritual and secular, the Vedas, the Upanishads, the epics, poetry, art, astronomy, medicine and so on were all inspired by these mountains. It has been aptly said that the mountain is mountain to us but what we are to the mountain?

Healing at the Mount Kailash

Hindus, Buddhists, Jains and followers of the oldest Tibetan religion Bon believe that by going to Mount Kailash as pilgrims and circumambulating, they will cure any illness. They firmly believe that the power of Mount Kailash will wash away our sins. This belief is recorded in the Ramayana, asSherring and Longstaff described in their book, *Western Tibet and the British Borderland*:

"There is no mountain like the Himalaya, it is Kailash and Manasarovara that, as the dew dried up by the morning sun, so the sin of the world dried up at the sight of the Himachal."
According to the Vinaya Pitaka (འདུལ་བ་ལུང་),

གང་ཞིག་དད་ཅིང་མོས་པའི་སེམས་ཀྱིས་རྒྱ།
སངས་རྒྱས་མཆོད་རྟེན་ལ་ནི་སྐོར་འདོད་ན།
འཇམ་བུའི་རྒྱ་པོ་གསེར་གྱི་གྲངས་ཆད་ནི།
སྟོང་ཕྲག་བརྒྱ་ཡང་དེ་དང་མཉམ་པ་མིན།

The result of taking circumambulation is,
Whoever out of faith and devotion,
Wants to meditate the water as Buddha's temple
Then it is even not same amount as world rivers,
Of a hundred thousand gold.

Every site around Mount Kailash has a peculiar appearance, charm and beauty of its own. Each hour as we pass along the ritual route, presents a fresh scene and each turn reveals new glimpses and beauties of the mountain in more grandeur.

To the Buddhists and the Bons, Mount Kailash and its circumambulation route is a sort of terrestrial projection of their religious mandala, each circuit a single turn of the wheel of life. It is believed that circumambulating Mount Kailash by proxy on our behalf could be achieved by paying fees to the fitter poor people.

In the opinion of Swami Pranavananda, the universities are responsible for young people lacking the enthusiasm for mountaineering and adventure in our modern time. In his opinion, the universities should now encourage and inspire young students and finance them to go to the Himalayas on educational and health tours. Marco Pallis in his book, *Peaks and Lama,* writes:

"The Himalayan germ, once caught, works inside like a relapsing fever, it is ever biding its time before breaking out again with increased virulence." Now all young people of the world need an excellent guide, not to show them the route around Mount Kailash but to provide excellent spiritual guidance to attain the healthy atmosphere of spiritual goals.

Gifts from Mount Kailash

People who cannot visit Mount Kailash can receive souvenirs from people who have visited there.

1. Mount Kailash Incense (གངས་སྤོས།). A high-altitutde variety of scented creeper generally known as Gang pos grows around Mount Kailash on pebbly ground at a height range of 5,333 to 5,151 meters. This high quality scented herb is dried and used as auspicious incense. This herb is generally found in the upper part of the Namreldi valley.

2. Water from any side of Mount Kailash, ideally water from Tso Kapala and water from Gauri-Kund.

3. Sacred earth from Kapali comes in various forms. A white substance called skusa (སྐུ་ས) in Tibetan is brought from the northern foothills of Kailash, and used as Mount Kailash

vibhuti 4. The maroon earthly substance found from hot springs known as Tirthapuri is taken as Bhamsmasura's bhasma (གཤས་རིའི་སྐུ་བཅག). As Devi's gift, the pilgrims take the yellow ochre from the Sindura hill at Tirthapuri.

I have mentioned about the caves, monasteries, footprints, idols, and numerous holy sites situated on the pilgrim routes to Mount Kailash.

I have endeavoured to make a detailed description of each and every place that trekkers, researchers and holy pilgrims can visit during their pilgrimage to the sacred mountain.

Readers can note the places of auspicious association I have described. When there, they will observe the palpable piety of their fellow circumambulators.

TRIP GRADE

The trip to Mount Kailash and Manasarovara Lake is moderate to rigorous.

SEASON

Best season to make the trip is May through October.

CLOTHING

The climate around Mount Kailash is unpredictable and can be extremely hot and cold. During sunny days, if you expose any part of your body to the heat of the sun in summer, your body may be burned. But with the change of season, the weather becomes very cold. Your feet may suffer the ravages of frostbite if you walk in shade and on the snow without proper shoes or good woollen socks. There will be terrifying winds from the beginning of November up to the middle of May. Owing to snow on the mountain, your eyes may become inflamed. To avoid damaging your eyesight, you must wear sun glasses. If you lose your sun glasses, the local remedy is to rub your eyes with fresh snow. It is necessary to carry warm cloths, especially from October to April. Padded clothing is the best for trips at altitude. Having a changes of warm clothes for will help you on the trek, such as warm shirts, trousers, sweaters, down jackets. It is necessary to have good raincoats while circumambulating. Those who wish to circumambulate the outer circuit, October through April, should take woolen and down clothing and comfortable hiking boots are essential.

ALTITUDE SICKNESS

I have mentioned earlier that Mount Kailash is situated at altitudes of the great Plateau of Tibet of 13,000 feet (4000 metres) above the sea level. The area has virtually no trees, and you have to take portable fuels for cooking. Visitors and trekkers may suffer discomforts due to altitude sickness during the trip. The best way to avoid it is to acclimatize slowly, drinking plenty of water and thin black Tibetan tea, chew something eatable like dried cheese, chewing gums and dried fruits such as apricot and grapes and so on. One should also refrain from engaging in physically exhausting activities during the trip at high altitude.

Mount Kailash lies beyond the mighty walls of the great Himalayas. In ancient time, Mount Kailash virtually inaccessible for any one wishing to reach it from the plain of India in the south. It was only in the middle of the twentieth century that people learnt that there are many routes connecting Mount Kailash with the outside world. In olden days, people chose three main routes to reach Kailash. In old first entry point to Mount Kailash and Manasarovara Lake from the east crossing Kyirong (སྐྱིད་གྲོང་) was via Nepal. The pilgrims proceeded to Mount Kailash along the valley of Martsang Tsangpo.

The western approach, on the other hand, is from Kashmir and Kagzhung of Ladakh, India. The most direct pilgrim route was straight from the south, traveling to Darchula right on the Western Nepal - India Border. This route involved trekking through Almora and crossing into Tibet by one of the high passes like Niti, Lamkiya Dhupra, Kungri or the most direct and popular Lipu Lekh pass which is situated at approximately 5,060 meters altitude.

In pre-1959 days, people crossed the border and entered into Tibet and found themselves comfortably in Ngari, Western Tibet; this was ruled by the Dalai Lama's viceroy generally known as the Garpon (སྒར་དཔོན) risiding at Gar Phuntsoktse in Ngari. His power was like that of a State Governor of India today. Local powers were entrusted to the District Governors (རྫོང་ དཔོན, rDzongs-dpon). These officials were generally stationed at the more prominent community centres like Purang which was one of the districts. The Dzongpon (rDzongs-dpon) of that area lived approximately 11 miles (17 kilometres) from the Lipu Lekh pass. The District Governors normally came from Lhasa, the capital city of Tibet. This district is located 1,229 kilometres from Lhasa and approximately 58 kilometres from Mount Kailash. In the olden days, orders from the government were relayed to the local administrators along the high roads. The Lhasa-Gar Phuntsoktse highway passed through a beautiful spot situated on the marshy plain separating the sacred Mount Kailash from the twin lakes (Manasarovara and Rakshas Tal). An official stationed there was called Barkha Tazam, because he presided over a staging post where the rider carrying the official mails changed their mounts.

Now situation has completely changed, and Kailash is accessible by vehicles from different big cities of Tibet as well as from neighboring countries. These days foreign tourists can drive from Kathmandu, via Kodari, Nepal (seven to eight days by four-wheel drive). One can also go to Lhasa by bus from Kodari to Lhatse in Tibet, and from here, one can hire car to drive to Mount Kailash. One can fly from Kathmandu to Nepalgunj (40 minutes) and Nepalgunj to Simikot (30 minutes). From Simikot, one has to make trekking to Sher, a border village in Purang district of Ngari. It will normally take five days for slow trekkers. One can get a car and drive to Kailash via Manasarovara Lake. It takes two to three days.

In the olden days, there were no guides for tourists going to Mount Kailash. There were no lodges or eating places along the route. Now, there are plenty of guides at Dharchen with a police post stationed over there to check situation during the trading season.

In the table below are the details of the motor route from Kathmandu to Derchen, a Tibetan town just below the Mount Kailash, which goes to the sacred mountain and the lake via the western route crossing Martsang Tsangpo, passing beautiful scenery.

While proceeding along this route, one will cover a distance of 1,311 kilometres. You will not be covering the major big ancient cities or monasteries of Tibet, however.

Starting Place	Arrival place	Distance between the places (km)
Kathmandu	Barabesi	87 km
Barabesi	Dam (Kodari)	37 km
Dam	Nyanam	30 km
Nyanam	Dingri	150 km
Dingri	Shelkar	70 km
Shelkar	Lhatse	90 km
Lhatse	Saga	293 km
Saga	Drongpa	145 km
Drongpa	Barkha	387 km
Barkha	Derchen	22 km

For tourists and true lovers of Mount Kailash and Manasarovara Lake who wish to make pilgrimages to Kailash after visiting Lhasa and surrounds, there are two motorable routes for the trip to Mount Kailash. The western route covers a distance of 1338 kilometres only and the northern route covers 2021 kilometres. The northern road is 683 kilometres longer than the western road but people normally prefer to make their trip to Kailash along northern road, as it is the much comfortable route, especially during the summer and the spring. Even in winter, the road almost always remains open and it is easy to drive across the open vast plateaus chasing wild ass. Travellers pass through the most wonderful nomadic areas, where they can see the high mountains of Northern Tibet and its high plateaus. They pass through a few little Chinese built towns. From Lhasa to Lhatse, the route is the same and you pass through Gyantse and Shigatse. Both of these cities are famous and old with ancient forts. Tashi Lhunpo monastery is in Shigatse. From Lhatse, the roads go in different directions. Those who are traveling the southern road normally face an uphill task, as they have to cross many rivers without proper bridges and have to pass through vast sandy riverbanks. Since Mount Kailash and Manasarovara Lake are situated in a remote region of Western Tibet, which the Chinese Government has made into a restricted area, foreign tourists need a special permission from the regional office at Singe, Ngari. So, it is advisable for the foreign tourists to go through the northern road. The details of northern road from Lhasa to Derchen town are as below,

DEPARTURE PLACES	ARRIVAL PLACES	DISTANCES (KM)
Lhasa	Gyantse	250 km
Gyantse	Shigatse	90 km
Shigatse	Lhatse	151 km
Lhatse	Raga	241 km
Rage	Tsochen	242 km
Tsochen	Gyertse	260 km
Gyertse	Gyegyal	370 km
Gyegyal	Singe Town	112 km
Singe	Montser	237 km
Monser	Derchen town	68 km

The route to Mount Kailash from Lhasa along the southern road passing old Tazam is given appended below,

DEPARTURE PLACES	ARRIVAL PLACES	DISTANCES (KM)
Lhasa	Gyantse	250 km
Gyantse	Shigatse	90 km
Shigatse	Lhatse	251km
Lhatse	Saga	293 km
Saga	Drongpa	145 km
Drongpa	Barkha	387 km
Barkha	Derchen	22 km

Today, Mount Kailash and Manasarovara Lake have become very famous, and many people want to visit the holy mountains. Nature lovers come here to enjoy the picturesque and high snow landscape. Western tourists also come to Kailash and Manasarovara through Pakistan via Xinjiang's old city of Hari. This road winds through ten snow-covered mountains in the Kunlun ranges. Almost 1,000 kms of the road are 4,000 meters above sea level and about 130 kms of the road are 5 000 meters above sea level. This road, which connects Ngari to Yecheng, Xinjiang, was built and opened to traffic in October 1957. One can really enjoy the beautiful scenery of the high and sharp Rocky Mountains. The road passes through different cities on the way from Hari to Derchen. This route is mainly used for local transportation between Xinjiang and Ngari and by tourists who are coming only from Pakistan. [Editor's note: access to this route depends on international visa availability and local travel restrictions and is not generally used by westerners.]

DEPARTURE PLACES	ARRIVAL PLACES	DISTANCES (KM)
Hari	Yekhring	249 km
Yekhring	Matser	249 km
Matser	Chehren Dophen	456 km
Chehren Dophen	Domar	136 km
Domar	Ruthok	149 km
Ruthok	Singe Town	117 km
Singe Town	Montser	237 km
Montser	Derchen	68 km

This route has a total distance of 1,661 kilometres.

Another very important road to Mount Kailash starts from New Delhi, India via Jang La of Purang district in Western Tibet and has a distance of 866 kilometres only. This road is for Indian nationals only. Foreign nationals are not allowed to take this route because this area fall under the protected areas. The details of this road are given below.

DEPARTURE PLACES	ARRIVAL PLACES	DISTANCES (KM)
New Delhi	Almora	395 km
Almora	Barinag	68 km
Barinag	Darchula	78 km
Darchula	Gharyang	157 km
Gharyang	Jang La	38 km
Jang La	Purang	18 km
Purang	Derchen	112 km

It is very important to keep contact with Tibet Tour office stationed at different places.

Mountaineering

It was said that Milarepa who was entirely free from sin and had the power of flying along a ray of light reached any top of Mount Kailash in the tenth century. Since then there is no record of any holy person or other human having made any attempt to climb the Holy Mountain and it remains an untouched holy place. However, in the early 1920s, British mountaineers took an interest in climbing in Tibet. In 1925 Hugh Ruttledge was appointed Deputy Commissioner of Almora on the border with Ngari.

In July 1926, Ruttledge came on official business, accompanied by his wife, to meet the senior Garpon of Ngari, at Gar. The Garpon was away so the pair decided to make the Kailash circuit together. Mrs Ruttledge was first Western lady to make a circumambulation of Mount Kailash. The pair performed a remarkable trekking feat, covering 600 miles (970 kilometres) on foot. The British couple were the first known western people to make the crossing of Trail's Pass between Nanda Devi and Nanda Kot. While circumambulating Mount Kailash, Hugh Ruttledge studied the accessibility of ascending the mountain via the north face, which he estimated was 6,000 ft (1,800 metres) high and he found "utterly unclimbable". He also explored a way to find an ascent route specially from via northeast ridge, but could not do it due to the shortage of time. Colonel R.C. Wilson who accompanied Hugh Ruttledge on trip along with Sherpa Satan had also trips to find feasible ascent route from the other side of Kailash. To some extent they found a feasible ascent route from the south-east ridge of Mount Kailash. In 1936 an Austrian author, geologist and climber Herbert Tichy was in Ngari, attempting to climb Gurla Mandhata. He met one of the Ngari Garpons whom he asked whether Kailash was climbable; the Garpon replied, "Only a man entirely free of sin could climb Kailash. And he wouldn't have to actually scale the sheer walls of ice to do it he'd just turn himself into a bird and fly to the summit". In the mid-1980s, the Chinese Government offered an opportunity of climbing to Rienhold Messner, which he declined. In 2001 the Chinese Government granted permission to climb the peak of Mount Kailash to a Spanish team. However, due to international disapproval, the Chinese authorities withdrews permission to climb the Holy Mountain. Regarding the banning of the Spanish team, Reinhold Messner said, "If we conquer this mountain, then we conquer something in people's souls, I would suggest they go and climb something a little harder. Kailash is not so high and not hard". It is true Kailash is not high. But it is the root soul of four major world religion, Kailash will remain the holy mountain as long as the sun, moon and stars remain in sky.

Manasarovara Lake

❖

Ngari in western part of Tibet is famous for being the main source of water in the world. It is said that twenty million years ago, Ngari was at the bottom of the sea. In time, the water dried up and the land of Tibet emerged in Tibet. As a matter of fact, the Ngari emerged in its present commanding position in Central Asia. Its appearance has been described as an epic in the long history of the formation of the earth's crust. Tibet is caught between two approaching land masses in which the seabed buckled into a series of long parallel mountains. The tops of those mountains were worn down by the rain-bearing winds blowing up from India, while the intervening depressions were filled up with alluvial silt, creating the great Jangthang, the vast northern Tibetan plateau that stands at an average elevation of 4,900 meters above sea level. Tibet has still many large lakes, while major global rivers are flowing from Tibet.

This is the highest plateau of Tibet where inhabitants live. Most of the high land is still virgin, and many people view it as the world's last bastion of "clean land" free from pollution. A major part of the land is covered with rich flora and fauna, and some people call it Shangri la or a hidden land in Tibet. In the upper part of western Tibet many wonderful, unique and fascinating world famous high mountains stand and from those areas waters flow downwards. One only has to look at the clay forest stretching across a vast part of the region. It is said that Ngari alone has more than 70 lakes, scattered across the vast area like stars in the azure sky in the night, and there are also about 100 big rivers. The most noted and mysterious holy lake is Mapham Yumtso (Mapham gYu-mtso) meaning in Tibetan "Eternal and Invincible Turquoise Lake". In the real sense, Mapham means the undefeated lake due to its pure water and healing power. This holy lake lies at a height of 4588 metres (15,052 feet) above sea level, covering an area of 412 square kilometres and reaching a maximum depth of 90 meters (300 feet). It is situated 940 kilometres (580 miles) from Lhasa.

In Sanskrit, it is popularly known as Lake Manasarovara, and holds a significant and sacred position for different religions of the world. The water of this holy lake is pure and fresh because it is among the highest in the world. This lake is frequently and liberally endowed with both religious and mythological lore. Lake Manasarovara is the holiest, the most fascinating, the most inspiring, the most famous of all the lakes in the world and ancient lake that civilization knows. Burrand and Hayden wrote,

"The Lake Manasarovara was the first lake known to the geographer. The Lake Manasarovara is famous in Hindu mythology. It has in fact become famous many centuries before the Lake of Geneva had roused any feeling of admiration in the civilized mind. Before the dawn of history, Lake Manasarovara had become the sacred lake and it has remained so for four millenniums".

The beauties of the lake have been richly eulogized, particularly the rich color of its water.

She is majestically calm and dignified. She is like a real turquoise, a large one, set between the two mighty and equally majestic silver mountains, Mount Kailash to the north and Gurla Mandhata (25,355 feet or 7728 metres high) on the south. Her water is graded from a limpid blue near the shores to a deep emerald green through deep blue to the purest ultra marine as we approach the center. It is a heavenly blossoming forth, reflecting the resplendent golden rays of the waning sun or moon and the myriad pleasant hues of the vesper sky, or her smooth surface mirroring the amber columns or silvery beams of the rising sun and the moon, adding to her own mystic charm. Wonderful sunsets take place here when the world is aflame "with all the colors of fire." From the spiritual point of view, she has the most captivating vibration of the supreme order that can soothe and lull even the most wandering mind into sublime serenity and transport it into involuntary ecstasies. People even believe that to take a dip in Lake Manasarovara will cleanse all the sins committed over even a hundred lifetimes and emerge reborn and he/she shall go to paradise, bDe ba chen kyi zhing khams (བདེ་བ་ཆེན་གྱི་ཞིང་ཁམས།). On the shore of Lake Manasarovara and living around Mount Kailash an animals has no fear for their life as the visitors will not commit the sacrilege of killing them when they are on the holy ritual trip around Lake Manasarovara.

Buddhist scholars such as Ekai Kawaguchi, Lama Anagarika Govinda and John Snelling (The Sacred Mountains, P. 42) believe that Manasarovara was identical with the legendary Anovatapta Lake. Prior to the birth of the Buddha, his mother, Queen Maya Devi, had dreamed of being transported there by the gods and having a bath in the waters there. When her body was thus purified and she felt ready to receive him into her womb, the Buddha appeared from the direction of Kailash, was riding a white elephant and surrounded by five peaks. A different legend describes the Buddha and many Bodhisattvas sitting on lotus flowers floating on the surface of the lake that are not visible to mortal eyes. It is said that on the birthday of Lord Buddha, a rare and precious flower of Udum Wara'i Metok (ཨུ་དུམ་ཝཱ་རའི་མེ་ཏོག) a fabulous lotus of immense size, blossomed on the shores of this lake.

འཕགས་པ་བསྒྲུབས་པ་ལས། མ་དྲོས་མཚོ་ལ་སྐྱུ་བདག་མེད་གྱུ་ན། འཛམ་བུ་

གླིང་དུ་རྒྱུ་གླང་འབབ་པར་ག་ལ་འགྱུར། རྒྱུ་གླང་མེད་ན་མེ་ཏོག་འབྲས་བུ་འབྱུང་

མི་འགྱུར། རྒྱ་མཚོ་ཡང་རིན་ཆེན་གཟུགས་མེད་པར་འགྱུར། ཅེས་དང་འཛམ་

བུའི་གླིང་དུ་རྒྱུ་གླང་རྗེ་སྐྱེན་གཉིས་འབབ་ཅིང་། མེ་ཏོག་འབྲས་སྨིན་སྨིན་དང་

ནགས་ཚལ་སྐྱེད་བྱེད་པ། མ་རྫས་གནས་པའི་ཀླུ་དབང་ཀླུ་བདག་བརྟེན་གནས་
ཏེ། དེ་ནི་ཀླུ་ཡི་བདག་པོ་དེ་ཡི་མ་སྲུད་དཔལ་ཡིན་མཚོ་འདི་ཉིད་ཀྱི་ནང་དུ་
བསྐལ་པ་བཟང་པོའི་སངས་རྒྱས་ཞིག་ཀླུ་རྒྱལ་པོ་བྱུང་ཆུབ་སེམས་དཔའི་ཆུལ་
བཟུང་ནས་ཀླུའི་འགྲོ་བ་རྣམས་ལ་ཆོས་སྟོན་པ་དང་འཛམ་བུའི་སྐྱིང་དུ་རྒྱ་སྦྱོང་
དང་མེ་ཏོག་དང་འབྲས་བུ་དང་སྨན་དང་ནགས་ཆལ་ལ་སོགས་པ་ཀུན་སྐྱེ་
པའི་བྱེད་པོ་མཛད་པ་ཡིན།

We also believe that Zambu Trishing (འཛམ་བུ་ཁྲི་ཤིང་།, a fabulous fruit tree or the wish-fulfilling tree of God which produces the fabulous fruit of the Kalpadruma), grew from the middle of the lake and was in land of demi-gods with fruits grown in the heaven where the gods used to have the fruits. The Naga King, the divine cobra, and his subjects lived in this lake. They fed on the fruits of this giant Zambu Trishing that had fallen from the heaven. Some of the fruits of the great giant tree fell down into the water and sank uneaten into the bottom of the lake. It is said that it is there that it automatically transformed into pure gold. These beliefs are further substantiated with a coincidence: gold has been found near the northwest corner of the Manasarovara just south of Byiwu Gonpa (བྱི་བུ་དགོན་པ།). The Nepali adage which says of a lady that there is gold in Tibet but her ears are bare and naked may reference it indirectly.

Swami Pranavananda says there is a gold deposit extending from the shores of Lake Manasarovara right up to the Rakshas Lake. An earlier Tibetan government conducted mining in those places. It was at this very place where our ancestors mined the gold till 1900 CE but gold mining operations were eventually discontinued that year when small pox broke out among the miners, a plight attributed by the Tibetans to the wrath of the presiding deity of the mines. Consequently, the government ordered the mining to stop. During the last mining operations, the miners found one nugget of gold as big as three-year old dog (ཁྱི་ཐོང་པ།, Khyi Thonpa). Later on, a stupa was constructed at the site where the nugget of gold was found. The nugget was sent to Lhasa as a gift to the Dalai Lama but the Dalai Lama regarded its extraction as sacrilegious and His Holiness the Thirteenth Dalai Lama Thupten Gyatso ordered it to be returned. Later on, this mining area was named Golden Dog mining area (ཁྱི་རོ་གསེར་ཁ།, Khyiro gSerkha). This particular area is about a mile south of Byiwu Gonpa.

According to Hindu mythology, the sons of Brahma went to the north of the Himalayas and performed ritual austerity on Mount Kailash. At Kailash, they saw Lord Shiva and his consort Parvati. The sons of Brahma remained there for twelve long years absorbed in mortification and prayer. Due to low rainfall over there and lack of sufficient water, the Rishis could not take their baths for a long period of 12 years. They approached Brahma and prayed for his help to make a place for their bathing with sufficient water. Brahma with mental power prepared Lake Manasarovara for the sages as well as for all future human beings. We believe that this lake is created by a mental effort of God, the creator or Mana meaning "the Mind".

Hindus, Buddhists, Jains and Bonpos believe that those who drink its water will go to the heaven of their lords. Even animals drinking the water of Manasarovara will go to paradise. Its water is like pearls. With this belief in mind, modern people can look today at many hotels, restaurants and shops bearing the name of the same Lake Manasarovara.

The Skanda Purana of the Hindus says that as the dewdrops are dried up by the morning sun, so are the sins of human beings by the sight of the Himalayas, where Lord Shiva resides and the Ganga falls from the foot of Vishnu like the slender threads of a lotus flower.

It has aptly been said that there are no mountains like Kailash and no lake like Manasarovara.

According to our religious scriptures, this lake has been named Ma, meaning "Mother" and, thus it is the mother of all the rivers in the entire world. This lake carries its legends and the water from the lake can be used to rinse away the "five poisons" from the mind. The written account of Manasarovara Lake has been established over a long time. During the third century CE, Kalidasa, the great Indian poet, extolled its virtues in his book *Meghdoot,* "The Cloud Messenger".

The pilgrims who succeed in reaching Mount Kailash and Lake Manasarovara have to adhere strictly to the precepts laid down by different religious sects. One should pour water to purify all the sins one has committed during the time even of one's ancestors and worship one's own god. The Hindus worship Mahadeva (Shiva) in the form of a royal swan. The Buddhists worship and consider that Dechog (bDe-mchog), a tantric deity of Buddhist Samvara, is surrounded by the deities of Sky-walkers (མཁའ་འགྲོ།). Both the Mahabharata and the Ramayana tell of a White Mountain named Kailash in its several appearances. Those holy books also describe a lake called Manasarovara and references are also made in the Ramayana regarding Lake Manasa.

According to Hindu legends, there is in this lake the Lord Shiva and his beautiful wife Goddess Uma (Parvati), the daughter of the Himalayas who took a bath in it. According to the Buddhist religious texts, Dechog Kuyine (བདེ་མཆོག་གི་སྐུའི་ གནས།, bDe-mchog gi Kuyi gNas) is the home of gods. Lake Manasarovara enjoys a reputation for its charms and sacredness equal only to that of the holy mount Kailash. This lake is not only known for its purity but also for its large size, depth, altitude, visibility, beauty and serenity.

Over time there has been an increase in to search this holy lake; the movements of Indian religious emissaries, distinguished travelers, marauders, traders, and wandering sages and pilgrims beyond the northern high barriers have also equally increased practically every year. It was during King Ashoka's period in the third and second century BCE that unprecedented movement and greater contact took place between Tibet and India, increasing knowledge about Mount

Kailash and Lake Manasarovara. Furthermore, evidence was collected in India about the four greatest and largest rivers on the sub-continent, the Indus, the Sutlej, the Karnali and the Brahmaputra as emerging from the great mountains. All the rivers recognised as having originated in one corner of Tibet's distant high plateau beyond the Himalayas. In due course of time, the geographical knowledge on them also increased and further they detract the majesty and mystery of the world. Mount Meru assumed pure and abstract form and became identified with as the Mount Kailash.

Ever since the discovery of the ritual route to Manasarovara Lake by the great saint Gotsang Gonpa Dorje, visitors have appreciated this unique, fantastic and pure turquoise lake ithat is surrounded by extremely beautiful landscapes. The waves of the blue lake move smoothly across, and the distant mountains can be seen reflecting distinctly around the lake under the blue sky with white clouds. The surrounding area is so beautiful that people consider it as a fairyland of Tibet. According to a western travel book, Lake Manasarovara is described as "a jade pond in the west" of Tibet. It has attracted numerous pilgrims, domestic as well as overseas, both Buddhists and non-Buddhists, from all over the globe.

This lake is the holiest among the holy lakes in Tibet. The lake is situated at about 15 meters higher than its neighbor, Rakshas Tal, which is separated by a narrow isthmus of land. This lake is of an oval shape. Since the lake is situated at a high altitude, it freezes during the winter. This happens on the night of either on the 10th, 15th or 25th day of the 11th month of the Tibetan lunar calendar, or December every year, according to western calendar. Again, in April either on 10th, 15th or 25th day of the second Tibetan month, she melts into clear blue water. She remains frozen for a three and half month period every year, and we say that the Bodhisattva of serpent-king sat in meditation for the period of three and half months.

According to Vinaya Pilaka (འདུལ་བ་ལུང་།), there was no lake at this site in the beginning. A king who was as compassionate as a Bodhisattva ruled over Ngari. He wanted to get rid of the sufferings of human beings like illness, sorrows, decay and death. He sought advice from his religious master who asked him to give a public feast without any prayer material objects for a period of 12 years. The king accepted the advice ; while preparing a large amount of rice for the feast, extra water was added and a huge pit was created. The pit covered a vast area of land the boiled water filled. After twelve years, the heavy and rich feasting came to an end. On the following morning, the hot liquid from the boiled rice was turned into pure clean water, and since that very day, it has come to be known as the famous Lake Manasarovara situated on the roof of the world. Because the rice-cooking water was warm when it was turned into a lake, it is called "Ma-dros" meaning warm water, and is also called Mapham Yumtso (མ་ཕམ་གཡུ་མཚོ།, Mapham gYu-mtso), meaning "Magnificently Victorious" lake, because evil spirits never overcame the water-deity of the earth Naga King. We believe that the holy water from Lake Mapham Yumtso through its ever lasting purity washes away the sorrows of all mortal beings.

According to Norsang Opera (ནོར་བཟང་སྒྲུ་གཞུང་།), this lake is called "Pema Lhatso" 'A Precious Lotus Lake'. It looks as if it would mingle earth and heaven into an organic whole. According to ancient mythology, this is the fair lake of the western paradise on earth. According to some Pali and Sanskrit Buddhist works, Mansarovara is described as Anotatta or Anovatapta Lake , the lake without heat and trouble. In its center, there is a tree which bears fruit that is a panacea for healing all human ailments, physical as well as mental, and as such much sought after by gods and human being alike. The water can remove impending misfortunes, misery and drive away illness. This Anavatapta is described as the only true paradise on earth. It is also believed that a mighty lotus flower, as big as the seat of Amitabha Buddha, blossoms in the Holy Lake, and the Buddha and Bodhisattvas often sit on those flowers. Heavenly rajahansas (royal swan) live there singing their celestial melodies, as they swim around the lake.

Those with supernatural and spiritual powers consider the sand of the Lake Manasarovara as pure gold. While circumambulating the lake, Gotsang Gonpa Dorjee had visions that the holy sand of the Mapham Yumtso was gold dust not sand; Panchen Lobsang Chokyi Gyaltsen Rinpoche had a similar vision in the year 1618 when he was circumambulating the lake. He asked his attendant to bring two dre (ཟེ།) of sand from Lake Manasarovara. The attendant could not understand what his master was asking for, but since it was his master's order, he took only one dre of the sand and gave it to the Panchen Rinpoche when they were back in Tashi Lhunpo after successfully completing the trip to Mount Kailash and Lake Manasarovara. To their utter surprise, they found that it was not sand but pure gold. Later on, during the time of the Fourth Panchen Lama, a statue was made at Tashi Lhunpo and the same gold was used for gliding the statue of the late Third Panchen Rinpoche; it was found that it was of the purest form of gold.

Lake Manasarovara has yet another important link with Lord Shiva. The golden swans were known to have been swimming on its surface. To further substantiate this view, we have, in fact, numerous species of golden birds living around this lake during the summer. Hindus believe it is the summer abode of the Hamsa goose; the Hamsa is an important element in the symbology of the Indian Subcotinent, representing wisdom and beauty.

Before 1959, thousands of birds used to lay their eggs on the shores of the Lake Manasarovara, as the environment was so calm and peaceful. Nobody was allowed to fish or kill the birds throughout the long history of Tibet until the Chinese occupation and their cruel and brutal rule. In olden days during the hatching period, the Governor of Ngari used to appoint watchmen to ensure that the young birds grew up peacefully without any disturbance from wolves, vultures orhuman beings. The watchmen were responsible for the safety of the young birds. They used to receive their salary from the local government of Ngari.

Yet another interesting legend in the Tibetan religious books states that a Zambu-Trishing, the giant fruit tree or the king of trees, grows from this lake. It is again said that we, ordinary people, may not be able to see the existence of the Zambu tree due to our ignorance. Only people with supernatural powers could see of its existence. The fruits of the tree fell down into the lake with the sound "Zam" and so the region became known as Zambuling, the Jambudvipa of the Hindu Puranas.

According to the Kagyud scriptures, their great teacher, saint and scholar Pyen-Ngalingpa (སྤྱན་སྣ་གླིང་པ), had put his saffron robes on a branch of the Zambu tree while he was making prostration. Since his fellow monks could not see the tree, they said that their master had placed the robe onto the thin air. While circumambulating Lake Manasarovara, Panchen Lobsang Chokyi Gyaltsen prayed to Mount Kailash and Lake Manasarovara and offered a scarf and hung it upon a branch of the tree, which remained there for a whole week. People were surprised to see the scarf hanging in an open sky for a week without any visible objects that could hold the scarf.

People who have not paid even a single visit to it would find it difficult, if not rather impossible, to appreciate the grandeur of the holy lake and to visualise the diverse aspects of beauty and charms that she presents during the different seasons of the year. In order to realize and fully appreciate the holiness of Lake Manasarovara, one has to actually spend extended time on the shore.

Monasteries around the Lake

❖

In order to make the place more holy for us, our great religious teachers and saints constructed religious institutes at different beautiful locations around the lake. There were eight Buddhist monasteries around the lake, wherein our Buddhist monks spent all their lives striving to attain the sublimity of the eternal silence of Nirvana. Their locations described below.

Seralung Monastery (སེ་ར་ལུང་དགོན་པ།), is located to the east of Mapham Yumtso. This area is the holy place prophesied by the tutelary deity yidam of Gyawa Gotsang Gonpa Dorje who had spent a number of days meditating at this place before he proceeded to Mapham and Mount Kailash. This monastery was founded by the great Lama Kunchok Gyudzin of Drigung Kagyud and was financed by Namru dPon for the purification of his sins committed during the wars with Ladakh in 1679-1684. It is located at an area resembling a lotus with eight petals. This area is also called the eastern gate of Lake Manasarovara.

Nye-go Monastery (མཉེས་འགོ་དགོན་པ།) is on the south-east side. Ngorchen Kunga Lhundup of the Sakya founded it in 1018 CE. When Jowo Atisha was on his way to circumambulate the lake, he admired the location and spent a few more days there performing religious rituals and meditation. He made small statues, and placed them secretly in the lake bottom for the benefit of future generations. Later on, Ngorchen Kunga Lhundup went on retreat in this area and had a holy glimpse of Guru Padmasambhava. Kunga Lhundup first built his monastery above the cave Drak Chodphun in front of Fragrant Incense Mountain (རི་སྤོས་དད་ལྡན།). During the rule of Ladakh by the Namgyal dynasty from 1633-1683 CE, the old monastery was destroyed. Later on, the lamas of the monastery shifted it to a new place for safety from the enemies. Alas! It could not be saved during the Chinese Cultural Revolution and this new monastery too was totally destroyed by the Chinese forces.

Lho Trugo Monastery (ལྷོ་ཁྲུས་སྒོ་དགོན་པ་) is situated at the South Gate of Lake Mapham Yumtso. Before opening of the whole lake after the three and half months' frozen period in winter, this very small part of it would melt earlier because this aspect of the lake was on the southern side. It is called Lho Trugo (Lho Khrus-sgo, The Purification Gate of the South). This monastery is owned and managed by the Gelugpa sect. This is the oldest and biggest of the eight monasteries. The number of ordained monks living in this monastery was the largest among the monasteries around Manasarovara. But due to Chinese occupation and the impact of the Cultural Revolution in Tibet, this monastery was extensively destroyed. The rich artifacts inside the monastery, such as statues glittered (glistened?) with gold and silver, along with the priceless ancient painted scrolls (ཐང་ཀ་), were taken away to China; and remaining were burned. So hundreds of religious scriptures were destroyed during the so-called Cultural Revolution.

Gotsug Monastery (འགོ་འཛུགས་དགོན་པ་) is situated in the south-west of Manasarovara Lake. The Lake provides fine caves on her shores near Gotsug ('Go-'dzugs) Gonpa for hermits, for fine camping grounds, and good sites here and there for Tibetans to construct monasteries and houses. According to the history of this monastery, Gelong Jinpa Norbu of Purang Shenphel Ling established Gotsug Monastery as prophesized to him by a water-diety of Mapham Yumtso. Gotsug means "start" as taught by the gods. This area is also purified and sanctified by great saint and hermit Gotsang Gonpo Dorjee. This was the starting point for the discovery of the Mount Kailash and the Lake Manasarovara. Gonpo Dorje stayed at this place before he proceeded to Mount Kailash and Manasarovara Lake to create the ritual circuits route for the benefit of beings. The area is warmer than the other parts of the lake. He undertook a retreat a holy cave for about a month praying and performing religious rites for a successful discovery of the circuit around the mysterious Mount Kailash and Manasarovara Lake. In due course of time, many hermits dwelt in this cave for a long time but no one could establish a permanent monastery there. So, it was only Gelong Jinpa of Purang who was able to found the monastery at this holy spot in the middle of 19th century. Although this place is holy for Kagyudpas, the religious sect of the monastery is Gelukpa. This monastery too was destroyed during the Cultural Revolution under the Chinese occupation. This monastery is situated towards the southwest of Lake Manasarovara. When the Chinese colonialists relaxed the rigid anti-Tibetan religion policy in Tibet and the Chinese Government declared that they were seeking facts from truth, this monastery was rebuilt, and a few monks are living now in the monastery, and it is now open for the visitors.

Byiwu Monastery (བྱིའུ་དགོན་པ།) is situated on the western side of Manasarova Lake. In spite of the existence of the hot spring nearby, the Byiwu hillside area is very cold. The area has beautiful caves situated on the corner of a mountain. It is said that Guru Padmasambhava spent 54 long years here offering his magnificent and wonderful religious service to the Tibetans on his way to Ngayab Ling (རྔ་ཡབ་གླིང་།) in the year 876, the year of the Fire Monkey, in order to defeat demons and evil spirits, and he also spent a week in a cave performing prayers while sanctifying and purifying the land. Guru Rinpoche left his footprints on a stone there. Palden Drukpa Dingche Dhondup Thongmon owns the monastery. The Chinese destroyed this very monastery too as part of their evil destruction of monasteries in Tibet so as to erase the very essence of Tibet itself.

Jakyib Monastery (བྱ་སྐྱིབས་དགོན་པ།) is situated to the north-west side of Manasarovara Lake. This monastery was originally founded above the cliff on the bank of Lake Manasarovara. It is a holy place where Lord Buddha along with his 500 disciples spent a week in the various caves located at the site, as mentioned in the Gangri Karchag on Mount Kailash and Manasarovara. We regard those cliff caves as an area prophesied by Lord Buddha himself. This place is called Golden Cliff Caves (གདན་པ་གསེར་གྱི་བྲུ་སྐྱིབས།). We can see the footprint of Lord Buddha along with his 500 disciples on the rocky cliffs at this very place.

Later on, during the glorious period of the Kagyud sect, many hermits were sent to various religious holy places to do retreats for the benefit of sentient beings and their material prosperity. During the time of Drigung Chen-nga Lingpa, all the caves throughout Ngari were filled with great saints from the Drigung Kagyudpa tradition. Chen-nga Lingpa along with his 500 hundred hermits spent many years hearabouts, and most of the caves and holy places were owned by them, and they built monasteries around Mount Kailash and Lake Mapham. The holy places practically belonged to Drigungpas. Tsang Nyon Heruka, a great saint from Drigung, who set up a monastic institution, made the Drigung order flourish in this area too. During the invasion by an alien power under the Ladakh king, the old caves were destroyed and many of them were washed away by the lake water or fell down into the lake, and non-virtuous persons and non-believers occupied and stayed in them. The remaining four to five caves nearby the monastery set up by the Drigung were finally destroyed during the Chinese Cultural Revolution. The holy caves and monastery have not been repaired so far, and there are no yogis in retreat there. The only holy article remaining at the place is a sandalwood statue of Guru Rinpoche, and mental alloy statues of Vajrapani and Lord Buddha.

Langna Monastery (གླང་སྣ་དགོན་པ།) is situated at the side of the mountain projecting like an elephant trunk. It is thus called Langna (gLang-sna) Monastery. Nyenmo Kunga Samten spent a number of years at Mount Kailash performing rites and meditating, and he also established a small shrine there. Later on, his reincarnation Lama Kunga Lodoe Nyingpo of Drigung Kagyud built a beautiful and a unique monastery resembling Drigung Yangrigar in Central Tibet. During the massive destruction of cultural institutions of Tibet under the cruel Chinese occupation, this beautiful monastery was also demolished and destroyed. In 1986, this monastery was rebuilt and now is open for a few monks and one can visit the monastery while one is on the pilgrimage circuit to the lake.

Bonri Monastery (བོན་རི་དགོན་པ།) is situated in the north-east of Manasarovara Lake. According to the legend, Milarepa arrived at Mount Kailash and the Manasarovara Lake in 1093. The local deities and serpent king of kLu (Naga) gave a warm reception to Jetsun Milarepa on his arrival at the holy lake. Those areas had belonged to the Bon religion since its founding. It is said that during that time, Naro Bonchung, a famous Bon scholar was living around Mansarovara and Mount Kailash. He was acting as the head of his religion and had a great reputation, as people believed that he had attained mystical supernatural powers. Naro Bonchung felt unhappy and had uneasy time on the arrival of Milarepa at his area, as Milarepa also had great fame having already earned his reputation. The two great religious scholars first met at the shores of Lake Manasarovara. Naro Bonchung first asked Milarepa who he was and where he was proceeding.

"I am Milarepa, proceeding towards Mount Kailash for meditation," replied Milarepa. Naro Bonchung said, "Oh! Kailash and Manasarovara are like you, having great fame and reputation far and wide. Whatsoever the reputation and majesty may be, the mountain and the lake belong to me. If you like to stay at those areas for a longer period, you have to convert yourself to my religion", Naro Bonchung commanded.

ARRIVAL OF MILAREPA AT MANSAROVARA LAKE

Milarepa, the great yogi and poet of the period having fully attained supernatural mystical magic power, naturally did not accept the commands given by Naro Bonchung.

"Lord Buddha himself prophesied that one day Mount Kailash would fall under the sway of the followers of the Dharma. My own great teacher Marpa prophesied to me to proceed to this holy mountain. It is good that you Bonpos have lived here for years. Now, if you wish to live here, you have to renounce your faith and convert yourself into a Buddhist. If you do not like to become Buddhist, you have to leave for another place." This is what Jetsun Milarepa told to his opponent Naro Bonchung.

In order to resolve the differences, Naro Bonchung responded, "Oh! You and I will have a mystical contest and whosoever wins the contest will have the right to own and to control the area. The loser should leave the sacred mountain to the winner of the contest." The Bon master Naro Bonchung then first demonstrated his mystical magic power by straddling Manasarovara Lake. He started singing inflammatory songs as given below,

གངས་དཀར་ཏི་སེ་སྨྲ་ཆེ་ཡང་།
རེ་མགོ་ཁ་བས་གཡོགས་པ་གཅིག
མ་ཕམ་གཡུ་མཚོ་སྨྲ་ཆེ་ཡང་།
ཆུ་ཉིད་ཆུ་ཡིས་བཤགས་པ་གཅིག
མི་ལ་རེ་པ་སྨྲ་ཆེ་ཡང་།
མི་ཉན་གཅེར་ཉལ་བྱེད་པ་གཅིག
དེ་ལ་ཡ་མཚན་ཆེ་རྒྱུ་མེད།

The English rendering of the above stanza is roughly translated as follows:

Although the Mount Kailash is famous, its top is covered by snow.

The Manasarova Lake is famous the water cuts off its water.

Although Milarepa is famous, he is an old man without proper clothes.

So it is all not to be surprised.

Naro Bonchung boasted of his own supernatural mystical prowess while using abusive language to his opponent Milarepa.

In reply Jetsun Milarepa without making Mapham Yumtso smaller or without enlarging his own body, covered the lake and made also a counter inflammatory song as below,

ཁྱེད་ཡོངས་སུ་གྲགས་པ་མི་ལ་ངས།

བློ་བྲག་མར་པའི་བཀའ་སྒྲུབ་ཕྱིར།

ཏེ་སེ་གངས་ལ་སྒོམ་དུ་ཡོང་།

རང་གཞན་དོན་གཉིས་སྒྲུབ་པའི་ཆེ།

ཁྱོད་སྤྱ་ལོག་ཅན་གྱི་བོན་པོ་ལ།

བཀའ་མཆིད་གཏམ་ལན་སྒྲུ་ཡིས་འདེབ།

གངས་དཀར་ཏི་སེ་སྒྲ་ཆེ་ཡང་།

རི་མགོ་ཁ་བས་གཡོགས་པ་དེ།

སངས་རྒྱས་བསྟན་པ་དཀར་བ་ཡིན།

མ་ཕམ་གཡུ་མཚོ་སྒྲ་ཆེ་ཡང་།

ཆུ་ཉིད་ཆུ་ཡིས་བཅགས་པ་དེ།

ཆོས་རྣམས་བཞེན་པར་བསྒྲལ་བ་ཡིན།

མི་ལ་རས་པ་སྒྲ་ཆེ་བ།

གནང་འཛིན་སྒྲུབ་པ་ཐོན་པ་ཡིན།

སྤྱང་སེམས་གཉིས་ལ་དབང་བསྒྱུར་བས།

 སྣ་ཚོགས་རྟ་འཕུལ་སྤྲིན་པ་ལ།
འཛམ་གླིང་རི་རྒྱལ་ཏེ་སེ་འདི།
སྤྱིར་སངས་རྒྱས་བསྟན་པ་ཐམས་ཅད་དབང༌།
སློས་མི་ལ་བརྒྱུད་དང་བཅས་པར་དབང༌།
ཁྱེད་ལྷ་ཕོག་ཅན་གྱི་བོན་པོ་རྣམས།
ཚོས་བྱེད་ན་ཀུན་ལ་ཐན།
མི་བྱེད་རྟ་འཕུལ་ང་ཆེ་བས།
ཡུལ་ཕྱོགས་ས་ཆ་གཞན་དུ་སོང༌།
སྤྲ་ཡང་རྟ་འཕུལ་འདི་ལ་སློས།

The English translation roughly is,
    I am famous Milarepa,
    To fulfill the order of Lhodrak Marpa,
    Came to the Mount Kailash to meditate
    For the benefit of both myself and all sentient beings,
    You, follower of Bon, and holding false views,
    I reply with songs.
    The Mount Kailash is famous,
    Its top is covered with snow,
    It shows the Buddhism is white.
    The Manasarovara is famous,
    Its water cut off by water,
    It is sign of smooth flourishing of Buddhism.

    I, famous Milarepa,
    With no good clothes,
    The sign of holy yogi who has attained Enlightenment,
    Fully purified internal mind and control over it
    Could perform all sort of magic.
    Not surprise to the goddess of world,
    Earthly king of the Mountains, the Mount Kailash,
    In general, it is for all Buddhist followers,

But in particular, it is for the followers of Milarepa and
  Kagyud.
You, the follower of Bon and holding false views,
If you follow Buddhism, it is beneficial for all
If not, I am more learned in magic.
You go to another place.
Yet look at my repeated magic.

With those powerful words, Milarepa lifted the whole of the
lake on his fingertip without causing harm to the animals living
in it. The Bon master Naro Bonchung was highly impressed by
the performance of Milarepa. He accepted the outcome of this
first and initial magic contest. He insisted on having many more
miracle contests to be held between them later on at the Holy
Mountain, but Naro Bonchung was always defeated, as he had
fewer magical powers than Milarepa. Due to his arrogance, Bon
master Naro Bonchung was finally subdued. Naro Bonchung
humbly requested to Milarepa that his followers be allowed to
circumambulate the holy mountain and lake in their own way.
He also requested to Milarepa to provide a place from where
the followers of the Bon religion could see Mount Kailash.
Having won the mystical tantric magic contest, Milarepa
agreed to grant the first request made by the Bon master and in
response to the second request Milarepa picked up a handful
of snow from the Kailash and threw it on to the summit of
Mount Taklha situated nearby. Since then, this mountain is
popularly known as Bonri Mountain (བོན་རི།), Mountain of the
Bon religion.

Khedup Lobsang, the great follower of Je Tsongkhapa
(rJe Tsongkhapa) of the Gelukpa tradition from the Guge
region spent a number of years at Mount Kailash. He built the
monastery at the peak time of the spread of Gelukpa tradition
in the Guge region in Ngari during the reign of His Holiness
the Great Fifth Dalai Lama. He constructed his monastery at
the base of Bonri and the followers of Gelug from Mongolia

provided the financial assistance. The Chinese also destroyed this monastery during the Cultural Revolution in Tibet. This is also one of the monasteries, which has not yet been repaired or rebuilt after the Chinese occupation. Jiwu (ཇེའུ) and Trugo (ཁྲུས་སྒོ) are the well-known monasteries surrounding the holy lake. Lho Trugo monastery and the area around the monastery is considered to be the most respected, holy and the pure bathing place. Buddhists believe that the water from the Lake Manasarovara can wash away our accumulated sins or five malignancies of the human mind like greed, anger, craziness, sloth and jealousy. These disturbing evils can be removed from our consciousness. People take holy dips into Manasarovara. They wash their heads, faces, feet and hands as soon as they arrive at Lho Trugo. As a result, the holy lake is crowded with people who come from a long distance to take bath or take a dip every year. People also regard the water from Lake Manasarovara as nectar and take it back home for their relatives and friends. Lho Trugo monastery is owned and managed by the Gelukpa sect, and it is the biggest and the oldest monastery of the Gelukpa in this area.

According to our texts, there are four gates for bathing or taking dip for people who circumambulate the holy lake, one at each of the four compass points.

Gate of Lotus Bath is in the east, on the bank of the holy lake situated at Tsewalung, a mountain resembling a lotus with eight petals flashing the five colors of golden sands.

Gate of Sweat Bath is in the south, located below the five mountain peaks where natural incense grows.

Gate of Filth-Removing Bath in the west, is situated at the place called Five Filth-Removing Peaks where varieties of natural cloth washing powders are available.

Gate of Belief Bath in the north, is situated at the lake side of the mountain where numerous statues and letters inscribed on stones and statues imprinted on stone are found by those people who are faithful to the religion.

The turquoise blue lake stretches majestically over the huge cradle of the western Tibetan plateau and is located at a heavenly height of 14,950 feet (4556 metres) above sea level. Pilgrims who wish to make a ritual circumambulation around the holy lake by visiting all eight Buddhist monasteriescover a distance of 96 km. If one circumambulates only the lake, the distance is 84 km. Usually, the pilgrims will take more time by visiting all the monasteries on the shore. Orthodox pilgrims perform 3 or 13 circuits of Manasarovara.

Generally, circumambulation of this lake, takes four days. Some pious pilgrims do prostrations around (Sashtangga Danda Pradakshina) the lake, and it generally takes 28 days. Some rich but sick people who cannot perform the parikrama themselves pay poor people and coolies to do the circumambulation on their behalf. We do the parikrama for the benefit of washing away sins and earning good merits during our lifetime. We also undertake the circumambulation for the benefit and peace of the souls of our departed relatives. The pilgrimage circuit of the lake is much better than that of Mount Kailash. In days gone by, there were no bridges over the rivers for crossing, nor were there any lodging facilities for the travelers. The pilgrims had to carry all their necessary amenities on their backs or on animals. Normally, in the old days, during winter, there were more pilgrims to Lake Manasarovara than to Mount Kailash, as it was much easier for them to make that trip. There were, however, more pilgrims to Mount Kailash during summer. (Mount Kailash is 26 kilometres from Lake Manosarovara.)

Heinrich Harrer, author of *Seven Years in Tibet*, and the Austrian mountaineer who escaped to Tibet in 1944 during the Second World War with is friends, had caught a glimpse of the Mount Kailash when he and his companion arrived at Barkha Tazam. As a mountaineer, his instincts urged him to make the parikrama but the officials stationed at Barkha Tazam blocked his path. They were obliged to proceed straight on their way. Gurla Mandhata was majestically reflected in the turquoise water of Lake Manasarovara and Heinrich Harrer and his companion took a bath in the icy water of the sacred lake in the interests of hygiene rather than spiritual purification. But the beauty of the sacred lake and the surrounding region deeply impressed him. He wrote, "This is certainly one of the loveliest spots on the earth".

Lanka Tso or Lanka Lake

Buddhists have less often travelled to the golden Lanka Tso (la-nga-tso). La means mountain pass, nga means five, and tso means lake. The Lanka Tso means a lake with five mountains. Hindus it as Rakshas Tal. This lake is situated only 5 kilometres from Lake Manasarovara. According to Swami Pranavananda, the circumference of Lanka Tso (Rakshas Tal) is about 124 kilometres (77 miles). Its east, south, west, and north coasts are roughly 29, 35, 46 and 13 kilometres (18, 22, 28.5 and 8.5 miles) in length respectively. It measures approximately 27 kilometres (17 miles) north to south and and 21 kilometres (13 miles) east to west at the maximum point. The modern geographer says that the lake has 275 square meters and is always frozen during winter. During spring times, the ice melts as the weather warms. In the Bon religion, this lake is called mTso Mule (མཚོ་མུ་ལེ།).

As its name implies, the Rakshas means demon. An adage states,

 སྲིན་ཡུལ་ལང་ཀ་པུ་རང་ན། །
དུག་མཚོ་ནག་པོ་མེ་རེ་རེ། །

In the land of demon Lanka Purang,
There lies Poisonous Lake.

Rakshas Tal was originally the abode of a demon popularly known as Gonpa Bengchen (དགོན་པོ་བེང་ཆེན།), and as such, nobody drank water from. It was regarded as a haunting place of the demons, and the place of one of the most notorious of them, Ravana, the kidnapper of Sita in the epic Ramayana, after he had done his penance to propitiate Shiva. Some visitors have claimed to be able to detect a sinister quality in the atmosphere around the lake, although others have found it as beautiful as its eastern neighbor. Interestingly, this lake cannot boast of having a single monastery and has no circumambulation route. Some scholars talk of a deep symbolic significance between these two lakes. In their view, Manasarovara represents the light, positive, masculine disposition whereas Rakshas Tal, the dark, negative and feminine one. We believe in yab and yum, like the yin and yang in the Chinese philosophy of Change (I-Ching). It may be coincidence but the water of the two lakes flow into one to another by way of a channel that pierces the intervening isthmus (མཚོ་སྐྱེང་པན་ཆུན་སྨེལ་མཚམས་ཀྱི་སྐྱེང་ལག་ནར་མོ།). Thus, making the water of Rakshas Tal pure and drinkable.

In 1942, Swami Pranavananda with great effort circumambulated the lake from 13th to 16th October. He had a thorough look at this lake and made careful observations. As far as my knowledge goes, he was the first human being who circumambulated this lake. So the route seemed to be very rough. He described that sometimes he had to jump over boulders at several places since there was no regular path along the shore, but the changing scenery was the most thrilling, romantic and beautiful. Due to unfavorable weather, he made the circuit in a great hurry. He said that each hour revealed a fresh scene and each bend presented a new glimpse of the mountain and variety of views. Early in the morning, the lake was so rough and raging with high roaring waves that the whole surface was white with foam. After a few minutes, he found himself walking around a gulf and the water in it was emerald-green and so perfectly still that the tiniest pebble in its bed and the swimming fish could clearly be seen and perfect stillness reigned supreme.

From one vantage point, the Mandhata mass could be observed on the south with its giant heads piercing into the azure hues and at another place, the water in a bay was frozen and holy Kailash with its majestic and sublime serenity reflected in it, as if in a mirror.

According to our legend, long, long ago there used to live two golden fishes in Manasarovara Lake. One day, a fight occurred between them. One of the golden fish from Manasarovara Lake defeated his opponent, and when the defeated fish tried to run away, the victor pursued her making a carved channel into the nearby lake. The course, which the golden fishes took, was the present channel of the Ganga Chhu, the holy water of the Manasarovara flowed out of it through the course taken by the golden fishes into Rakshas Tal. In such circumstances, the water of Lake Manasarovara was enabled to flow into Lake Rakshas. Since then waters of this lake were sanctified and made drinkable. This is the only outlet through which the excess water of Manasarovara flows into Rakshas Tal. Generally, during the rainy season, this outlet is 12 to 30 metres (40 to 100 feet) breadth, 9.5 kilometres (six miles)long in its winding course and 120 to 180 centimetres (2 to 4 feet) in depth.

In comparison to Manasarovara Lake, this lake is lacking the warm spirit environment and is more uncomfortable than Manasarovara. Having colder weather and less hospitable in winter, in consequence, it is abandoned in favor of the more hospitable and agreeable climate of the Lake Manasarovara. The Rakshas Tal has three islands.

Even Dr. Sven Hedin said that he had seen three, the lake is completely frozen.Lochato islet is a rocky island having the appearance of a tortoise with the neck stretched out towards a peninsula on the southern shore. The distance between the neck of the island and the shore is nearly 1.6 kilometres (1 mile). Like every islet in Tibet, the islet is home for birds during the summer. There are heaps of white stones with Mani slabs on the top of the hill called Labtse (ལབ་རྩེ།).

Another islet is called Topserma (སྟོབས་མེར་མ།). A walled house in ruins now was situated on the eastern part of its hill, and it was, at one time, a meditation centre for a lama from Kham, who had pursued his spiritual discipline there alone for about seven years. It was sometime in the beginning of this century. We do not have the name of the lama from Kham, but it was probably Golog Sertha Rinpoche who meditated there; he built a monastery at Ribo Tsegye, (རི་བོ་རྩེ་བརྒྱད་དགོན་པ།) in the northwest of Lanka Lake. This island is completely rocky and like the Lochato, it is a much larger islet. This island is situated about 1.6 kilometres (1 mile) from east to west and about 1.2 kilometres (three-quarters of a mile) from north to south. The southern part of the island is named Tonak. Both the islets are accessible to us when the water turns into ice during the winter. An islander comes out to the shores of the island and goes back to the island. During his visit, Swami Pranavananda found the walled house in ruins and also outside a small clay image of Avalokiteshvara. He was the first non-Tibetan to visit the island of Rakshas Tal.

Lama Anagarika Govinda describes Manasarovara and Rakshas Tal as the solar and the lunar symbols respectively. "Manasarovara is solar, light and masculine; Raksha Tal is lunar, dark and feminine. It is said that an occasional overflow of water from Manasarovara Lake into Rakshas Tal is a sort of "sexual intercourse" between the "bridegroom" of Manasarovara and the "bride" Rakshas Tal. Any long absence of water flow into the channel is believed to be an ill omen for the world, and any occasional flow of water from Manasarovara Lake into Rakshas Tal is considered to be a highly auspicious event for the entire world, according to popular belief.

Since they are located at high altitude, the weather conditions of Mount Kailash and Lake Manasarovara are generally cold, and the climate is harsh all year round. During the spring and the fall seasons, it is mostly cold and windy. This area falls in the wind zone of the Tibetan plateau with an average yearly wind velocity above 5 kilometres per second (3.2 mile per second), and gale force at least of grade eight. The gales blow for about 149 days in a year. Sometimes, there are hailstorms with big torrential rains and foggy weather. Sometimes, there is sun shining on the mountainous regions, melting snows and the rivers overflowing their banks creating havoc for the pilgrims and traders when they cross the big rivers that are on the way to their destination. During the winter, there is devastating snowfall and severe snowstorms too. So the weather is very cold most of the time and is unpredictable for pilgrims. During the cold and harsh conditions, people around the lake and Holy Kailash remain inside their homes like hermits in cave, praying for the well-being of human beings in the world.

The best season for pilgrims, inquisitive geographers, explorers and travelers is the months of May, June, September and October. Year after year, during these months, the pilgrims, explorers and tourists from different parts of the world flock to those mysterious areas like a swarm of geese rushing to their holy places of liking. Generally, it is very hard for travelers taking ritual trips and is still harder for a trip to Mount Kailash and Manasarovara.

Why it is a hard trip is clearly stated in our religious texts, as it is said that for during the journey after going northward from India and crossing nine Black Mountains, one will arrive at a "Snow Mountain", which is Gang Rinpoche (Mount Kailash). Lord Buddha told his disciples that from Gaya and Shravasti to the north and after crossing nine Black Mountains, there is Gang Tise (Mount Kailash), and beyond this, there is a mountain called sPos Ngad-Idan. Lake Manasarovara or "magnificently victorious" lake is in front of the sPos Ngad-Idan range.

During the rainy season, pilgrims cannot travel along the holy shore. On the northern side, pilgrims have to go still higher up. All the streams and major rivers flowing into the lake make the water muddy and raise the water level higher. During the hot summer, snows from the high mountains melt and their flowing down at full speeds is dangerous and very furious, often becoming impassable after midday. On such occasions, pilgrims have to stop their onward journey and wait till the next morning when the high water level goes down.

Finally, the surrounding area of Lake Mansarovara and Mount Kailash is considered to be Mount Meru. This mountain is the source of all the life-giving waters of the world. The water flow starts from the city of heaven on the summit and later on divides into four great streams that flow down in the four cardinal directions to water the four quarters of the world. These rivers are named as rMa-bya Kha-baps River in the east, gLang-chen Kha-baps River in the south, Seng-ge Kha-baps River in west and rTa-mchog Kha-baps River in the north. These four rivers have their Sanskrit equivalents also, and the Hindus have their own mythology attached to their origins. The Tibetans named the four rivers after the four supernatural animals, the lion, the horse, the peacock and the elephant, as the mountains from which four rivers flow are thought to resemble these animals.

Four Major Rivers of Ngari

Ngari is well-known for being the source of rivers in South Asia. The four major well-known rivers of South Asia are the Karnali, Indus, Sutlej and Brahmaputra. The reputation of the Lake Manasarovara as the mother of the rivers in the world was probably based on this. It is also the location of the sources of the four major rivers that flow into the Indian Ocean.

Our ancestors believed that only those persons who have supernatural powers like great saints and hermits can overcome such unnatural hardships to reach those areas. "Hardship" here indicates to the state of affairs in the lofty holy areas with cold and harsh climate, heavy snowfall with strong blizzards in winter with fewer inhabitants, long and arduous steep and lofty cliff passages and huge rivers gushing forth at full speed during the summer. Before the discovery of the pilgrimage circuit path for circumambulation, blessed and sanctified by our great lamas, the land was also infested with carnivorous animals. There were many robbers and dacoits along the way, hiding in the mountainous corners waiting for opportunities to rob the pilgrims. The Lord Buddha had blessed Mount Kailash and Manasarovara Lake to ensure the survival of sentient beings living on this earth during his lifetime.

Our great masters like Milarepa and Naro Bunchung with supernatural powers, however, lived in those places long before the discovery of the holy pilgrimage route around Mount Kailash and Manasarovara by the great Gotsang Gonpo Dorje. Most probably, before the arrival of Milarepa, the majority of Tibetan Buddhists even did not know the location of Mount

Kailash and the Manasarovara Lake. However, surely the Zhangzhungpas knew the location of Manasarovara Lake. Princess Sadmakar, a sister of King Srongtsen Gampo went to Zhangzhung as a queen of King Limikya (Li-mi rKya). She spent her time at this beautiful place playing with the fish of the lake. She met Ma-chung (rMachung), the messenger of her brother King Srongtsen, at the shores of the lake. I am quite sure that the Bonpos knew the lake pretty well. The Tibetans, following Tibetan Buddhism, did not go to these holy areas till Gyawa Gotsang spent his time there from 1213 to 1217 A.D. He discovered the route and circumambulated around Kailash and the lake for the benefit of people from neighboring countries. Later on, an unbroken chain of saints from the Kagyudpa sect came to this place and spent their lives at the Mount Kailash. Hence, Mapham and Kailash became a holy place for the Kagyudpa. Later on, lay people started going there for pilgrimage and began to undertake ritual walks.

According to a Tibetan proverb, "Ngari is the land of holy places, U-Tsang is the land of Dharma and Dokham is the land of high Lamas", because in Ngari, the most mysterious Mount Kailash and Lake Manasarovara are situated and people go on pilgrimages to there to accumulate merits. The biggest Buddhist monasteries are located in and around U-tsang. The high lamas of Tibet are born mostly in Dokham.

Nature lovers can really spend their time and money well here, in order to enjoy themselves around those high, beautiful mountains, the clear turquoise lakes, mountains, rivers, stupas in the rosy dawn, and the sun shining over the land. Whilst looking at scenery in the vastness of nature, one can have peace of mind. For those persons who know the real essence of the holy mountain and lake, it is worth spending time to circumambulate and meditate in the area for the betterment of themselves as well as other people both in the present and the future. So many of our great masters renounced their life and became ascetics, spending their entire lives in this holy area in search of the real truth.

Buddhists maintain that herbs capable of curing all the ills of mind and body abound in this earthly paradise. The environs of Lake Manasarovara have a similar therapeutic reputation, being endowed with many kinds of curative herbs as well as with springs believed to have healing powers.

Normally, our pilgrims who return from Manasarovara bring the following holy objects as souvenirs or Prasads of Manasarovara Lake to their near and dear ones in their home towns.

Jema Na-nga (བྱེ་མ་སྣ་ལྔ།) is a sand which consists of particles of five colors, green, white, yellow, red and black. Tibetans believe that this sand contains gold, silver, turquoise, iron and coral. The pilgrims pick this up from the East Coast, where it is found in thin layers on the ordinary sand for a distance of about five kilometres (three miles). We generally eat this sand, as Prasad of the Lake. This sand is much heavier than ordinary sand.

Davnam (སྤོས་སྣ་ལྔ།) is a variety of the scented Artemisia plants that grow all around Lake Manasarovara. The lake incense (mTso-spos) grows everywhere upto an altitude of 3,030 meters. Pang po herbal root incense grows a little to the east of the Lake Manasarovara and it can be had in small quantities at Lho Trugo Monastery too.

Smooth pebbles or Ku-na lnga (སྐུ་སྣ་ལྔ།) of various shapes and colors, mostly self-printed images of gods and deities, are picked up from the shores. They are kept either for the purpose of puja or for inside our amulets as charms.

Bul na-nga (སྦུལ་སྣ་ལྔ།), is a smooth white earthly particle. It is believed that when we wash our hair and hand with this object the sins that we have committed are washed away.

Last but not least the dried fishes are taken as gifts. Tibetans do not kill fish, but since small and big fishes are found around Manasarovara Lake, left there on the shore by the high tides and big dashing waves, as they died and drifted to the shores, these dead fishes are picked up and dried in the sun, properly preserved and taken by the pilgrims. These dried fishes are very helpful during the delivery of babies.

Both the traditional founder of the Bon religious scripture and the Hindu Purana has given detailed descriptions of the rivers.

The four great rivers rising in the highlands of Western Tibet flow through different places before joining the ocean. These rivers originate from the high mountains flowing in the four directions from Mount Kailash. They are named after the supernatural animals in paradise, as the rivers gush forth from the four high mountains projecting as the mouths of the animals. We, therefore, call them by the name of these four animals. An ancient civilization was established on the banks of these rivers. These rivers flow downward slowly, paying due respects to Mount Kailash and Lake Manasarovara before mixing with the Indian Ocean. Different religious books tell different stories on the meaning of each river as to how and why they are called by the names of animal and their significances, and purposes to the human society.

Let me now deal here with the mountain guide (གངས་ རི་དཀར་ཆག) book written by Drigung Chetsang Kyabgon in 1896. He based this book *Gangri Kharchag* on the book previously written by the Fourth Zhamar Chodrags Yeshi Rinpoche in 1504. This book is in verse. The other famous guide books are written by mKhas-pai rNa-rgyan and by Drigung Zhabdung Chodrags who lived from 1595 to 1659. Their approach is more scientific as to the different starting sources of the rivers, and the places they pass through like mountains, plains and gorges, valleys, villages, different towns of Tibet, and finally mingling with the ocean after passing through various cities in India and Pakistan. I will also give the names of oceans where these rivers come to mingle.

According to Vinaya Pitaka, these rivers are the Ganges, Sindhu, Sita and Pashu. They are described with their names in different contemporary literature as below,

Name (in Tibetan)	Name (English translation)	Sanskrit	Present	Direction
Glangchen Khababs	Flow from the Elephant Mouth	Ganga	Sutlej	West
rMabya Khababs	Flow from the Peacock Mouth	Sindu	Karnali	South
Senge Khababs	Flow from the Lion Mouth	Indus	Indus	North
rTa-mChag Khababs	Flow from the Horse Mouth	Pashu	Brahma putra	East

Gangri Karchag says that a stream flows from Gang Rinpoche into Lake Mapham (unconquerable lake). From Mapham Lake emerge four rivers circling the lake seven times before taking their respective courses in the four directions. It is also stated that the rivers do not circle seven times but that each river has seven bends before they actually flow down to the valleys. This is a sign of showing respect to Mount Kailash and Lake Manasarovara.

It was the British rulers in India who wanted to know what was going on in all around the territories immediately adjacent to the Indian sub-continent under their possession. They were keenly interested in opening up trade centers, and channels for the Christian missionaries. They were very much concerned to know the exact physical geography, locations and other political as well as relevant aspects of the area. The British explorers had paid special interest particularly to the twin lakes, Manasarovara and Rakshas Tal. In the old days, it was even thought that the great Ganges had its source in Lake Manasarovara. Eventually in 1808, British explorer Lieutenant

Webb, assisted by Captains Raper and Hearsey, made thorough exploration and fixed the main sources of the holy river on the Southern side of the Great Himalayas.

The source of Elephant River (གླང་ཆེན་ཁ་འབབས།) or Sutlej is on the eastern side of Manasarovara Lake upper part of the Ganglung Glaciers spring, known as Chumig Thongwa Rangdol, about 48 kilometres (30 miles) from Manasarovara Lake where the water emerges from a mountain that resembles an elephant's head. It flows through Titapuri, Kyunglung, Dawa, Thusam, Dongpo, Manam, Thoding, Chaksam, Tsarang Yardikuli, Rongjong Gyasam, Trinzam and Sibkyi Lhashon. From Sibkyi Lhashon, it crosses the Indian border in the region of Khunu Rampur village in Himachal Pradesh and then it runs through Simla. This river's has catchment system covers an area of 22,760 square kilometres before the river crosses the Indian border. Many tributaries join it in Punjab and Chandigarh. Finally, this famous river from Tibet joins the Arabian Sea in the eastern side of Pakistan. This river flows with sands of gold and the water has the potential of producing the best oxen and agriculture; it is a source of livelihood for everyone living along its banks.

The Peacock River (or Karnali) (རྨ་བྱ་ཁ་འབབས།) in the south starts from spring water in the rocky mountains of Lapiya pass at Purang 48 kilometres (30 miles) to the south-east of Mount Kailash and Lake Manasarovara. This majestic high mountain resembles a peacock head, and so it looks as if the river is coming from the mouth of peacock. The river flows through different villages of Purang, such as Khorchak village and Purang Zher village, the gateway where traders from all neighboring countries used to conduct businesses of exchanging their goods. This river a smaller catchment system, of 3020 square kilometres. This river flows with rich silver sand and it is said the water makes those who drink from it aslovely as a peacock. We normally consider that Purang ladies are more beautiful than other ladies in Ngari. After Purang, it crosses the Nepal border passing through Li-me and the Jumla region of Simikot, before entering into India through the state of Uttar Pradesh, then Bihar and West Bengal and to Bangladesh to its capital city of Dacca and lastly, it empties into the Bay of Bengal.

The Lion River (སེང་གེ་ཁ་བབས།) or Indus originates from the north-east foothills of Mount Kailash, about 100 kilometres (62 miles) from the Manasarovara Lake. The terrain of the riverhead looks like the mouth of a lion (or "Senge") and it is where spring water starts to flow down from the rock that looks like a lion's mouth. Hence, the name of the river came to be known as "Senge Tsangpo" or Lion River. It flows through Ngari town called Singe town like a piece of auspicious white khata loosely lying on the ground. A giant stone-lion stands at the center of the downtown traffic island facing towards the south-east. This is a symbol of the town in the modern time. This great Lion River flows through different counties like Dongpa Singtoe and Drichi. Then, it turns to Shungpa Martsen passing through Tsotsho, Gyamuk, Langchu, Gar Tashigang and Dechok covering an area of 27,450 square kilometres in its catchment. This river crosses the Indian border, passing through Leh , the capital city of Ladakh, Baltic, Hor and Kargyil area. From there, it flows into Pakistan through Islamabad before it finally joins the Indian Ocean. This river is rich diamonds and those who drink its waters become as brave as the lion. It is believed that people of Ladakh are braver than the rest of the region.

The Horse River (རྟ་མཆོག་ཁ་བབས།) or Brahmaputra is the most famous and the longest of all the rivers, and has many different names. It is called rTa-mchog Kha-baps meaning "gushing forth from the mouth of Superior Horse". Its source is at Jima Yungtrung glaciers about 100 kilometres (63 miles) south-east of Manasarovara Lake. While this river is passing through Bawa, Shungru and Tradun areas, it is known as Martsang Tsangpo, as we believe that this river has originated from the region of the Lake Mapham Yumtso. The eastern Horse River or Pashu is the longest, and has many tributaries of different sizes around the area that join it making it bigger, and stronger too. This river is called Horse River because it starts from the upland of the valley of Tsang Jema Yungtrung mountain range. From the back of the lofty cliff of Apchi, a rocky mountain that resembles a horse head, this river flows through its mouth, so it is called Horse River.

This river crosses the major part of Western Tibet and U-Tsang regions before it crosses the Indian border. This river is rich with sands of emerald, and it is also said that the water makes those who drink from it sturdy as a horse. Also, it is popularly held that people of Hor Doshod, where the river flows, have the best horses. It flows through the five Hor and the nine Dongpa countries. From here, it proceeds to Gacho through Rusar and Bawa. From Bawa, it turns towards the west and passes through Tradun, Shungru Drukha, Daga Dzong and Sangsang in Western Tibet. It enters into U-Tsang and flows west of Tashi Lhunpo Monastery at Shigatse.

This river passes further through Chaksam Chuwori at Lhasa, and it is here that the Kyichu River of Lhasa joins it, and it is known here as Yarlung Tsangpo till it enters into Indian after passing through Dakpo and Kongpo region. This great river of Tibet has the biggest catchment area in Tibet, and it covers an area of 240,480 square kilometres. When this river enters Assam State in India, it is called the Brahmaputra River and flows through West Bengal and then into Bangladesh through Dacca before joining the Bay of Bengal, where the Peacock River also joins it there. Lastly, all the four rivers of Western Tibet, which is a permanent source of water for all sentient beings, join the big ocean. All the scholars and learned persons unanimously agree with the same spirit and idea that the sources of water for the world are from these pure and holy four rivers of Tibet, coming from the four directions of Mount Kailash and Lake Manasarovara.

According to Gangri Karchag, it is said,
For the well-being of the four directions
Are the four rivers falling in the four directions of the mountain and the lake,
They originate from the Land of Snow, Tibet.
Their fame spread all across the world.

In a local parlance of Ngari area, it is said like this,

"Elephant River flows in the middle of Guge region,
The prosperity of Guge is thus emerged.
Lion River flows in the region of Ladakh,
The valor of Ladakh is thus obtained,
Horse River flows in the middle of Drosho region
The horses have thus grown skilful.
Peacock River flows into Purang Region,
The beautiful maidens of Purang thus emerged"

The verse suggests that the uniqueness of each river of Western Tibet is something the people have faith in.

The four great rivers of Mount Kailash still nourish millions of people these days. These rivers have succeeded in continuing to be the most vital resource for millions of human beings in the Indian sub-continent.

Pagong Lake

❖

Ngari is also known as a wildlife sanctuary. There are many big lakes in Ngari but not all are holy lakes. Some lakes are bigger than Lake Manasarovara, and many are saline. Ngari is also known for its beautiful landscape, and diverse wild species living among its virgin mountains. No wonder that wildlife lovers call it a paradise of precious wild animals. The specific location of the region, the lack of modern amenities and the ecological environment have preserved its age-old culture and the primitive status. The surrounding high snow-capped mountains also helps to preserve here some of the most rare world wildlife species in the world.

Due to its vast territory, high elevation, complicated topography, peculiar weather and numerous rivers and lakes, this part of Tibet's region is famous for many wildlife sanctuaries. For centuries, vast stretches of the land have remained virgin and their ecological environment has been well preserved in higher stretches of mountainous ranges. The Pagong Lake in Ruthok district is the biggest lake, and half of it is in the Indian state of Ladakh. This lake is very famous for its Birds' Islet. This lake is a wonderful home for different birds on the roof of the world during the warm season from May to September. The fascinating scenic lake adds yet another spectacular panoramic view to beautiful Ruthok County in particular and the Ngari region in general. This wildlife sanctuary for the birds of the world is situated in the northern part of the region. Local people call it, "Tso Ngangla Ringmo" meaning "Beautiful Long and Narrow Lake". This lake stretches 155 kilometres (96 miles) east to west, and it becomes narrow from the south to north, at its widest being 15 kilometres (9 miles) and at its narrowest only 40 metres (44 yards). The depth of this lake is 57 meters (187 feet) and the water of the lake is crystal clear. According to a geologist, "It is an island lake which has freshwater, semi-saltwater, and saltwater from east to west". The majority of the lake which lies in Ruthok district has fresh water, except a small portion, which is semi-saline. The Ladakh side of the lake has salt water and the local people extract salt from this part of the lake. There are numerous islands scattered around the lake in various sizes. These islets were habitat for birds prior to 1959. Also millions of fishes live in the lake free from human cruelty.

Due to its high altitude, the region of Ngari has no rich natural forests on its plateau. Hence, the island is free from trees. There are only a few bushes and grasses on the islet to shelter different species of birds such as the gull, also a small number of birds like gray ducks and cranes exist on the fish of the lake. When autumn comes, with cold freezing air from the high altitude of the Himalayas, the Pagong lake is ready to freeze or "to have a slumber during the winter. The birds that have migrated from warm lowland to the cool South Asian continent during the previous spring fly back to their warm winter sanctuary. It slowly closes its door and goes to sleep for the long winter months.

In the following spring season, the ice of Pagong Lake starts melting and opening its door to welcome the island birds. The warm beautiful air blows from the Bay of Bengal to the high region of Ngari and the beautiful creatures fly back to the islet producing numerous eggs and raising countless offsprings here. Being citizens of a Buddhist country, the people were sincere followers of Buddha's teaching and no one consumed eggs or killed any bird on the islet of Pagong Lake during the pre-1959 era. The best season for observing birds hatching eggs is from May to September. The lakes like Manasoravara Lake, Dramthang Tso, Gonggyue Lake, Ngalaringmo, Shawo Tso,

Gongle, and Darog Tso are famous for birds populations and hatching. Pagong Lake is situated in a pure land with natural surroundings. Perhaps, one may be tired of looking at birds in this world of untamed birds with their newly hatched young ones flying in the blue sky and white clouds over blue water. Their good fate created a home for them during summer seasons. The geographical formation of the area has separated the small islet from the outside world, and the bewitching beauty of the land is kept intact.

A Few Words about My Own HomeLand

God gifted my land with impressive natural fascination and its beauty makes my homeland special with so many peculiarities and uncertainties. Any one wishing to visit my homeland has to pass through great hardship, restrictions thrusted upon nowadays and prevailing current uncertainty prevailing. Yet, our extremely anxious yearning for our homeland to be in peace, happiness, freedom, strength and life are too stubborn and deep. The zeal and passion can withstand the trouble of traveling to that far distant region in the high mountains and half-explored nomadic areas called Ruchang, abound with highly rich natural resources.

This region is famous for its vast and dense population of wildlife species, and it is also known as the land of high quality antelopes and the land of natural conservation of wild animals and birds and other valuable species. The animals easily roam the natural high mountains, vast open land plateaus with clear blue lakes, and high gorge rivers that flow into Lake Ngangla Ringmo and Rinchen Shawo Yumtso, alongside the inhabitants, under the white clouds and blue sky. The wild animals and rare species have their own habitats according to the nature, and the altitude and have adjusted to living in the high mountainous ranges along with gentle people of the area. Some dwell in the high mountainous areas, and some in the warmer lowlands and plateaus. Numerous birds live in the region and some of them migrate to the region when the warm air from the Indian Ocean of the Bay of Bengal reaches the mountain area. Those beautiful and lovely birds that have fled back to their warm sanctuary during the cold days in Ruchang region now return to the beautiful lake to lay their eggs for eventual hatching. One can see the golden-colored wild yak (འབྲོང་།), the arrogant wild animals, strolling freely in the highest mountain ranges of Zula, Chenn Gagur and Dolung ranges.

The native nomadic people shift their dwelling to these mountainous ranges during the warm summer with their millions of domestic animals, seeking a good harvest of milk by making the highland grasses to the animals. The wild asses or Kyang (rKyang) leisurely graze along with our domestic animals on the grasses, and this can be observed in the major part of the nomadic pastural plateau except the high mountainous range. Big horn and alpine ibex are found in the low-lying hilly areas mingling with domestic animals. In summer, the surrounding mountains sparkle in the golden sunlight. Different types of birds cheerfully sing all around on the shore and (མཚོའི་རྫོ།) islets. The meadows are covered with numerous wild flowers that blossom around on the mountains and valleys making human lives happier. The area is filled with common antelopes and other wild life species that migrate to the region during the summer. They come from the upper parts of Ngari and freely graze on the lowland region of Sherkye area behind the dKabala Mountain and Wumbu Taling region of the Ruchung. The antelopes stroll in groups with their leader in the front, and when wolves and hunters kill their leader, they scatter and fail to reach their destination unless another group leader leads them. I am not sure about the status of the animals and birds existing in present day, but the landscape must be remaining same.

For nature lovers, geographers and soil scientists wishing to enjoy the season of mating and the birth of antelopes at Ngari, Damthang Tsaka in Horgunggyu area in Purang Country is the best area. The mating season starts in the ninth Tibetan month, normally October and the birth season is in the 3rd Tibetan month, generally in April. In the old days, no one was allowed to go hunting during the mating season, the Governor of

Western Tibet used to send wardens to protect the animals and birds for one month. Presently however, there is no restriction under the Chinese rule, and anyone, especially the Chinese, can kill the antelopes whenever they wish to do so.

Lake Ngangla Ringmo of Ruchang

Lake Ngangla Ringmo (དང་ལ་རིང་མོ།) "Beautiful long narrow lake" of Ruchung is situated on the north of the region, and its area is 507 square meters. It is not narrow like Tso Ngangla Ringmo of Ruthok County. Half of the lake is under the jurisdiction of Selhaquk and the Singkhor nomads, and the remaining part is under Ruchang nomads. Wawong River joins this lake from Shungpa region. This part of lake is known as a salt mining area, and the nomadic people mine countless bags of salts from here to send to trade centers at border areas or farmland regions of Ngari. This salt is carried to the trading center on the backs of male sheep and male yaks. The water of this lake is very clear and clean, and saltwater is only available at Wawon Thangtso where we used to mine the salt for our use and for trade.

The eastern side of the lake is narrow and the water is very clean. The Nangla Ringmo is situated 11 kilometres (6.8 miles) away from Rinchen Shawo Yumtso. The most unique feature of the lake is an islet standing elegantly in the midst of the lake. It is called mTsoritho meaning "Rocky Island in the lake" in Tibetan. In reality, it is not a rock, but a natural islet for the benefit of people as well as for birds during the summer. This mountain islet is mentioned in the Bon texts; during the Zhangzhung period this mountain islet was a holy place for the Bonpos and the great Bon hermits meditatedin the caves on the mountain islet. According to Bonpo text, once Khyungpo Legsmgon spent his life in one of these caves, meditating for the well-being of human beings.

The birds hatch eggs under stone boulders, bushes and in small holes, as this area has no trees at all. Since the islet is in the middle of the lake, there is no danger by predation of the young ones by other animals except eagles. The islet is filled with beautiful natural flowers rich grasses. Although the islet is not so big, its beauty and richness attract birds from around the world for hatching and safety. The majority of birds living in this islet are ducks, yellow geese and white cranes with black tails and heads. The birds migrate here during summer from Lake Pagong of Ruthok. This lake is calm during the winter just as the holy lake Mapham Yumtso and the whole lake is open to us. In winter, a few nomads live on the islet with their animals.

During the fall, we, the Ruchang nomads, used to live on the east and south side of the lakes. In winter, nomads live near the lake pitching their tents like stars in the sky in the vast surrounding areas. The surrounding landscape naturally adds an extra marvellous: to the view to Kawala ranges in the east and Gang Tsukgyan ranges in the north, Tsemo Khunglhung ranges on the south and the Dakrdo range on the west.

Lake Rinchen Shawo Yumtso of Ruchang
(རིན་ཆེན་ད་བོ་གཡུ་མཚོ།)

To the west of Lake Ngangla Ringmo lies another beautiful lake popularly known as Rinchen Shawo Yumtso (Rinchen Shawo gYu-mtso, Precious bowl of turquoise lake). According to a local legend, this lake is the sister of Lake Mapham Yumtso. The precious bowl of turquoise lake is 190 square metres in area. People consider this to be a holy lake where in one can find sheep, horses and yaks. On important days, one can clearly hear the beating of the drum and voice of musical instruments beneath the frozen lake during winter. Water of this lake is so pure that human beings drink its water during the warm season and also in winter. In winter, many nomads live along the south-east of this beautiful lake. During early spring and fall season, nomads live in the west, north and east side of that lake. This locked lake has no apparent drainage but locals believe that it has a passage under the earth and joins with Lake Ngangla Ringmo beneath. Not long ago, people of a clan called Ta who lived at Zhingsa (an agriculture area) during winter ignored the "opening" day or date of the lake ice melt on Lake Nganggla Ringmo and were, therefore, drowned drowned in the deeplake except for a few families who could cross the lake a day ahead. In the following year, autumn tents and light long sticks used for tent pillars were found on the shore of the Rinchen Shawo Yumtso. The mountains around the lake sparkle during summer in the golden sunlight, and the lake itself looks like a turquoise when the rays of the sun fall upon it. The brambles flourish between mountains and lake in the west with many natural fragrant flowers. The birds hatching their young under the thick forest of brambles are happily singing in different notes. It makes every one happy and relieved of their sorrow and keeps them away from worldly worries.

The major mountain rivers forming the upper part of the Ruchang like Kyigu Soyo, Tsewon, Gang Phunsum, Zula, Penthang, Chennghagur with many other small rivers, join one by one to the highland river of Panghlungh Marmo. This river flows between the foothills of the red rocky mountains in the north called Tsugde, a famous mountain belonging to a deity known as Tsugdeat North and the Thuhkrok ranges in the west and flows slowly into Shawo Yumtso. This is the only big river of the west that joins this lake. The landscape around this lake is so fascinating and magnificent that it relieves one of one's sorrows when gazing on the blue waves that gently move in the direction of the wind and reflect to the surrounding hills and valleys. The southern side of the lake has a thorny bushland filled with flowers in summer. Every lake in these high mountainous areas is a home for wild birds. This lake is also full of gulls and black-necked cranes, yellow geese and ducks. In the summer, the area is free from human crowds as we nomads move to the highlands, and it becomes the land once again for birds, antelopes and wild asses. The birds live in and life around the shore of the lake and antelopes enjoy around the lake grazing freely the green grasses of the beautiful Sherkyi and its surrounding areas.

The elegant white rock mountain with a tunnel in the middle, with so many caves in the rock, stands magnificently between the two lakes. Normally, the animals used to pass through this tunnel. It is believed that an animal disease called Gagnad (འབགག་ནད།) was stopped by the deity of this mountain. Even when the sheep suffer from this dreadful disease, we nomads take sheep to this mountain and when the animals pass through the tunnel, the next day the disease is cured. This white rocky mountain is considered as the kitchen of the deity of Kailash. According to local people, it is a fort of Great King Gesar. The auspicious and secret mountain popularly known as Kaba Lhatsen stands majestically to the east of this mountain. Below the Kaba Lhatsen Mountain, there is a pass popularly known as Kaba La. The Kaba Lhatsen Mountain is a secret home or fort of deity of a protector Ruchung nomads. The famous trade and tax route falls in the pass. On the top of the pass, there is a meteorite valley called Kabala Ting. The mountainous ranges are holy, and people considered the wildlife of mountains as the domestic animals of the deity of the area. In old days, guns were forbidden and no one was allowed to hunt wild animals living at the mountains. This is not only mountain where the wild animals live freely but there are many other mountains in the region where the animals used to live freely and they are the luckiest and the happiest.

Not far from the Kaba Lhatsen Mountain, to the west and in the midst of the ranges of Sherkye, there is a very special mountain. This mountain looks like the heart of a human being, a reddish mountain with white strips. The mountain is believed to be a fort of a minister of a protector deity; here the wild animals except golden-haired yak, "Drong", live safe lives, all animals freely mixed up with domestic animals. When they see us shouting, these animals stare at us with their heads tilted to one side and then they suddenly run away into the deep recesses in between the horizons. If one is not tired of seeing singing birds, freely grazing wild animals, smelling the fragrance of wild flowers and is looking for a soul stirring mystique and beauty, Ruchang is the best nomadic area to pay a visit. It is a land of nomads, a peaceful and tranquil nomadic area under the azure sky and white clouds, surrounded by snow-covered mandalas of mountains for pleasure and homely feelings. The nature is pure, free from modern pollution, gentle fresh airs blow from every direction. Wildlife lives a natural free life with people living around the areas as simple as nature herself, free from materialistic pollution of the mind. They live with beautiful surroundings of the mystique mountains, with lovely animals, sheep, yak, goats and horses in the remote north of Tadun County, to the east of Mount Kailash, West of Tapyer Tsaka the biggest salt land in Tibet and south of Gonphuk Lake. The people from our area cordially receive and welcome visitors from far and near as honored guests with warm hospitality. This is a perfect land where cups of mellow and fragrant butter tea, a glass of delicious and healthy milk from a 'Dri' (female yak) quenches the human thirst and revitalizes the human mind and body.

Words can not suffice to quench the thirst, only an actual visit there can make one experience the reality and harmony and symphony.

Mamig Gonpa, a brief history

The Mamig Monastery was built at the foot of an undulating mountain called Mamig Dakar fort for the local deity. The monastery was situated between the enchanting Ruchang and Singkhor nomadic areas where the land is semi-arid. This monastery was well over 300 years old before its complete destruction by the Chinese during the Cultural Revolution. Mamig means, "the eyes of Manasarovara Lake, and there are also two small lakes near the monastery. Mamig claims its origination in the Zhangzung's holy and reputed white rocky mountain known as "Mamig" Dakar, a white snowy rock wonderful mountain mentioned in the Bon religion which is situated here. It is a well-known holy place for retreat as well as meditation for practitioners.

There are two high mountains considered to be the palaces of the diety of Mount Kailash. One is the White Mountain (ཨ་མེག་ཟྲག་དཀར་), and the other is the Red Mountain (ཨ་མེག་བཙན་རེ་). Each mountain has one holy cave. The cave located in the upper area of the mountain is known as the palace or stronghold of the deity of the area. On the big rocky upland of this cave, one can clearly see a horse's footprint. Guru Padmasambhava paid a visit to these areas, and sanctified and blessed the mountains. It is said that he spent many months doing retreat in these caves and purifying the land for the benefit of human beings. Later on, Guru Rinpoche also subdued the evil spirits and turned them into deities for the protection of religion and human beings. He made extensive visits all through Tibet sanctifying the mountains, lakes and springs, and subduing the spirits and turning them into his subjects and protectors of the religion and human beings.

The great saint of Zhangzung, Drubchen Tsephung Dawa Gyaltsen, took up simultaneous retreats throughout his entire life in these two caves. Later on, when the great saint left for his heavenly abode, his holy body disappeared as a rainbow into the thin air, or in other words, he attained the rainbow body. Likewise, Dogon Tsangpa Gyare and Ngorchen Kunga Gyaltsen also took up retreats in these two caves.

When Gotsang Gonpo Dorje was taking up retreats in a cave in his home town, Tsipri, he was told in a dream by his deities to proceed towards Mount Kailash, being his place of duty for the welfare of sentient beings in these mountains. Thereupon, he rode upon a big vulture deciding that wherever the vulture would land he would do his retreat there. The vulture landed on the rocky mountain of Mamig. Gotsang Gonpo Dorje took up retreat in a cave there, and it came to be known as Gotsang cave. Later on, many saints blessed the Mamig area. Afterwards, Gotsong Gonpo Dorje also left for Mount Kailash and spent five years there. Although Milarepa visited Mount Kailash and Manasarovara Lake earlier, it was Gotsang Gonpo Dorje who stared the tradition of the Kagyud school of Buddhism all around Kailash and Manasarovara. Gotsang discovered the road for the ordinary people to go around Mount Kailash and Manasarovara Lake in 1213 and left Mount Kailash in 1217 after making one full circumambulation.

The altitude and climate of the area is also suitable for hermits. This area is perfectly located between the beautiful mountain of white Lhari (Deity Mountain) and red Tsenri (Spirit Mountain). Each mountain has a holy cave, and the Marmig Monastery is situated below the Gotsang cave in the middle of the two mountains. The monastery is accessible to the general population as well. The two caves at the two mountains are meant for highly religious people who can spend their lives doing retreats and meditation there.

The Sixteenth Gyalwa Karmapa also visited the monastery and the area for a short period. He was returning after spending a year in Dolpo, Nepal, and Kailash. Gyalwa Karmapa told his followers that it was very difficult to walk on this land as most of the stones bore the statues of holy images.

In the family of Sakya Ngagjang Rinchen Choephel, an intelligent son was born on the day of the 5th month of the Tibetan lunar calendar. This boy was born in the morning when the rays of the sun fell upon the high virgin snow-capped mountains. So, his parents gave him the name Gangshar Rangdrol. At the age of ten, he could read and write all the characters of Tibetan scripts and religions by himself. He learned the religious scripts from tutors or teachers, but it was only to remember what he had learned in his past life. Ngorchen Kunga Gyaltsen ordained him as a monk at the age of 11. His guru gave him the name Urgyen Chophel. He became a wise and learned scholar, and he spent most of his time in meditation and on retreat in the holy mountains and sacred springs performing holy rituals for the well-being of humanity. He also renounced all earthly materialistic longings. The nomads from Rujung and Singkhor area gave him overwhelming respect and also considered him as a great protector and a supreme spiritual teacher.

At this time, a highly religious saint visited these mountains and caves to undertake retreat and meditation. He was the great Drubwang Shabkar Tsogdruk from Amdo. At that time, he was on his way to holy Mount Kailash and Manasarovara Lake for pilgrimage. As a great meditator and practitioner, he spent a number of years meditating in this holy area of Mamig Mountain because the place was perfectly suited for meditation. From his holy tantric teacher, Jetsun Rinpoche, he learned tantra. Drubwang Shabkar Tsogdruk was the greatest and the holiest among the saints in Tibet in this modern time. Drubwang Rinpoche , also known as Jetsun Gangshar Rangdrol, the rest of his life in Ngari giving teachings to his followers. He has left behind many teachings that are very useful in our daily life. His most valuable teaching was "Instruction to the people of Ngari". He spent the entire time composing religious texts, meditating and giving teachings on tantra to his followers. He also went on pilgrimage to the holy Mount Kailash and Manasarovara Lake. Once he told his followers that since he was a hermit, he did not need any wordly materials for his living; he had a few belongings left and they were to be donated to the Tradun Monastery. The nomadic people from Ruchang and Singkhor became the faithful followers of Jetsun Gangshar Rangdrol. They paid high respect to him and he also blessed them accordingly. The nomadic people of those two places earnestly and fervently requested him that he should stay at these holy areas. They proposed to build a temple for the monks, and he should become spiritual teacher as well as the head of this monastery. The Rinpoche and leaders of these two nomadic groups came to the conclusion that they would together build a monastery on the holy mountain of Mamig, if the Lhasa Central government gave them permission. They sent request letters through messengers to Lhasa to seek the permission. There is a legend among the local people that to help them get permission, they presented a holy gemstone called Norbu Samphel to a Lhasa official.

It was during the time of the Fifth Dalai Lama that they got the permission. The Dalai Lama formally approved and officially put the royal seal on the approval letter for the construction of the monastery at Mamig. Jetsun Gangshar Rongdrol or Urgyan Choephel conducted sanctification rituals for the construction of Mamig Monastery. The simple monastery in this remote nomadic area was also built during the glorious reign of the Great Fifth Dalai Lama under the guidance of Jetsun Gangshar Rangdol Rinpoche. The expenditure for the construction materials were borne by the simple religious people of Rujang and Singkhor regions. After the successful construction of the monastery, young novices from the two nomadic areas were admitted, and the nomads agreed to meet the living expenditures. Thus, a Buddhist Sangha Mamig institution was established in this region, otherwise it would have remained an empty nomadic land.

The founder of the monastery Gangshar Rongdrol or Lama Urgyen Choephel passed away at the age of 63. His reincarnation Lama Kalsang Lodoe Gyaltsen passed away at the early age of 25. Other reincarnations were,

3) Lama Dungpa Kunga Tenzin
4) Dungpa Urgen Thongdol

5) Akar Tenpai Gyaltsen
6) Urgyan Sangpo
7) Urgyan Lhundup who expired at the age of 63 in 1925. Reincarnated lama Ngawang Lodoe Rinpoche could not escape from Tibet in 1959. He was captured by the Chinese People's Liberation Army while fleeing towards Nepal. During the Chinese Cultural Revolution, this monastery was demolished, but it was rebuilt by the lama with the support of the two nomadic peoples. Unfortunately, Ngawang Lodoe Rinpoche expired in year 2000 in Tibet at the same monastery.

We had four highly learned spiritual lamas at the Mamig Monastery in 1959. Ngawang Paljor was arrested by the Chinese at the border of Dolpo while he was fleeing from Tibet, and we have no news of his whereabouts even today. The case of Khenpo Tsondu is the same story. Lama Gyatso was arrested by China's People's Liberation Army along with Chikyab Tachung, the former head of Ruchang who was taken to Drapchi prison, where he expired in 1969 after Tsondu. Due to the destruction of all the available records we have no scholastic writings or life histories of the spiritual lamas. Fortunately, Lama Gyatso's reincarnation has been found in Bylakupee in South India and has been recognized by His Holiness the Dalai Lama. Presently, he is receiving religious teaching at Namdroling monastery in the same settlement.

The treasures of Mamig monastery

Initially the religious sect of this monastery is Nyingma, yet the monastery enjoyed a cordial relationship with other sects, especially Kagyud. As for the interesting holy areas in and around this monastery, there are two holy caves and four chapels, and a golden statue of Chuku Dorje Chang (which was the holiest among the belongings of the monastery). During the time of King Lang Darma, this statue is believed to have spoken out to the enemy to spare him and so it was saved at the time. The size of this statue is about one tritse, the height of one full hand from the elbow. There are two Buddha statues measuring about 20 centimetres (8 inches) and one big Guru Rabjampa statue, all of them made of Indian Sharli. Sharli is sort of brass popularly known as Ashtadhatu in Sanskrit, made with eight different precious metals. The Jowa Yeshi Norbu statue is about 30 centimetres (12 inches); it is said that during the reign of King Lang Darma, this statue also received punishment. There is also one Avalokiteshvara statue made of Sharli, a golden statue of Lagyud 21, also one statue of Padmasambhava made of Mantham. There were seven statues of reincarnated lamas of Mamig Monastery. Two were silver and four statues were made of brass with gold plating. One sandalwood statue of eleven-faced Jowo or Avalokiteshvara and there were also two more statues of Guru. They also had one statue of Gyalwa Gotsang Gonpo Dorje, plus a Sangye Rabdun statue among others in the monastery.

This monastery preserves many volumes of religious textbooks written in gold and silver. It has 14 volumes of Hundred Thousand Sutra texts written with golden letters and 16 volumes of same sutra text with silver letters. Two complete sets of the Hundred Thousand Sutra text are written with ink. About 20 volumes of various holy religious texts partly written either in gold or silver were also available for the monks for their study. For reading and studying religious scripts there were almost 300 volumes of Tantric and sutra texts also available for the monks.

There were numerous old and holy thangkas (painted scrolls) with gold print mostly offered by individual families in remembrance of their departed parents, children and relatives as per advice given by the respective lamas. All thangkas were lavishly gold-printed on ancient brocades.

They had three silver trumpets (རྒྱ་གླིང་།) and one big brass horn, a pair of conch shells and about twenty cymbals of different sizes. There were about one hundred sets of butter offering cups made of silver and water offering cups including one big silver butter lamp.

They also a Khikhor mandala (དཀྱིལ་འཁོར) in the monastery.

OBJECTIVE AND ACTIVITIES IN THE MONASTERY

Like every monastery in Tibet, the objective of monks and novices in this monastery was to learn religious scriptures and practice their teachings. They marked all the religious texts that they had to learn in their lives.

The monks also learned how to make offerings or prepare ritual cakes (གཏོར་མ།). The monks used to wake up early in the morning and memorize the scriptures. They took oral exams and written exams. The head lama or senior reincarnated lama taught the junior lamas and the heads of different sections of the monastery. The junior lamas, in turn, taught their respective hostel novices. They kept cordial relationships with other lamas and monks. The young novices and monks paid high respect to their seniors. In turn, juniors were treated as sons by their seniors. Every morning, all the monks including the senior lamas assembled in the main monastic hall for Morning Prayers that was more like liturgical acts for the monks. They had to perform Zhikro prayers in both the northern and eastern deity halls for one hundred repetitions. They also used to have great tutor and Monlam festivals there. On important religious days like Dukpatseshe, Gaden Ngacho, Saga Dawa or on death anniversaries of reincarnated lamas, they held special prayers. Special prayers were also held when there were offerings from the local people at the time of the death of their relatives. Of course, there were also pujas when people fell sick. In the main chapel, on the 10th of every month, they held prayers for the whole the day. On the 25th, they performed prayers in the Gonkhang or in the chapel of protector deities, and changed the butter lamp inside the main chapel and also in Gonkhang.

To be admitted as a monk in this monastery, one had to attain the full age of 18 years but not more than 60 years. If one became a novice below 18 year or more than 60 years, he could not receive a full share of alms from the offerings made by the local people to the monastery. They could not also hold high monastic posts in the monastery like that of abbot, disciplinarian, treasurer, store-keeper, procurer or caretaker of the main temple. Even so, there were so many over- and under-aged monks in the monastery. The limit of the number of the monks in the monastery was 60. Some monks and lamas used to visit remote and vast open nomadic areas by rotation to perform prayers for the nomadic families during times of death and sickness. They had to perform prayers on the occasion of child birth too.

INCOME AND EXPENDITURE OF THE MONASTERY

Since this monastery was located in a very remote and poor nomadic area, it was very poor in comparison to other monasteries in other areas. Yet this monastery owned over 100 yaks and 1200 sheep. The male yaks were kept for the transportation of salt and other nomadic goods upto the trade centers to get in exchange, wheat, barley, rice, sweets, clothes and other necessary goods from the Indian and Nepalese traders. These animals were reared by the nomadic people, and the exchange and purchase rates of collected butter, cheese and wool were fixed according to the existing rule of laws in the area. They could not collect more from the nomads who have kept the animals than was specified by the existing law. The nomadic people living around the monastic areas paid their taxes in dried yak dung. The monastery and nomadic people had to pay 53 silver coins to the Sera Je monastery. This monastery had to compulsorily purchase three loads of tea from the Lhasa Central government. The monastery had around 50 horses for riding and transportation to enable visits of the lamas and monks to the remote nomadic areas.

During the Chinese Cultural Revolution in Tibet, even the monastery in this remote area was not spared from ruthless destruction and was subsequently completely destroyed and demolished beyond recognition. But the monastery was rebuilt by the nomadic people living in the area with their meager resources and hard physical labor. Now the monastery is open, and a few monks are living here and it is open for the tourists too.

The Author

Born in Ruchang, Ngari of Tibet. Escaped in 1959 and sought political asylum in 1960. Graduated from Tibetan Homes Foundation in 1973 and obtain BA degree from Punjab University in 1977. He jointed CTA in 1977 as junior clerk and at the time of his retirement was working as general secretary rank. He served CTA from 15 June 1997 to 15 December 2012. He is an author of *History of Ngari, Rosary of white Pearl a youngster's ornament in Tibetan.*

Glimpse of Mount Kailash from Choku Monastery western side

Manasarovar Lake with Ripos Ngaden

Dolma with prayer flags overpass

Mana-
sarovar
lake from
eastern side.
Photo by:
Konchok
Choktsang

Ngari prayer flag hoisting ceremony in 2012

Manasarovar Lake, with clouds over the surrounding mountains
Photo by: Konchok Choktsang

Ngari Dharchen with the back of side of Mt. Kailash, view from Ser-shong thang. Photo by: Konchok Choktsang

Glimpse of Mount Kailash from northern gate.
Photo by: Konchok Choktsang

Map of the pilgrimage route

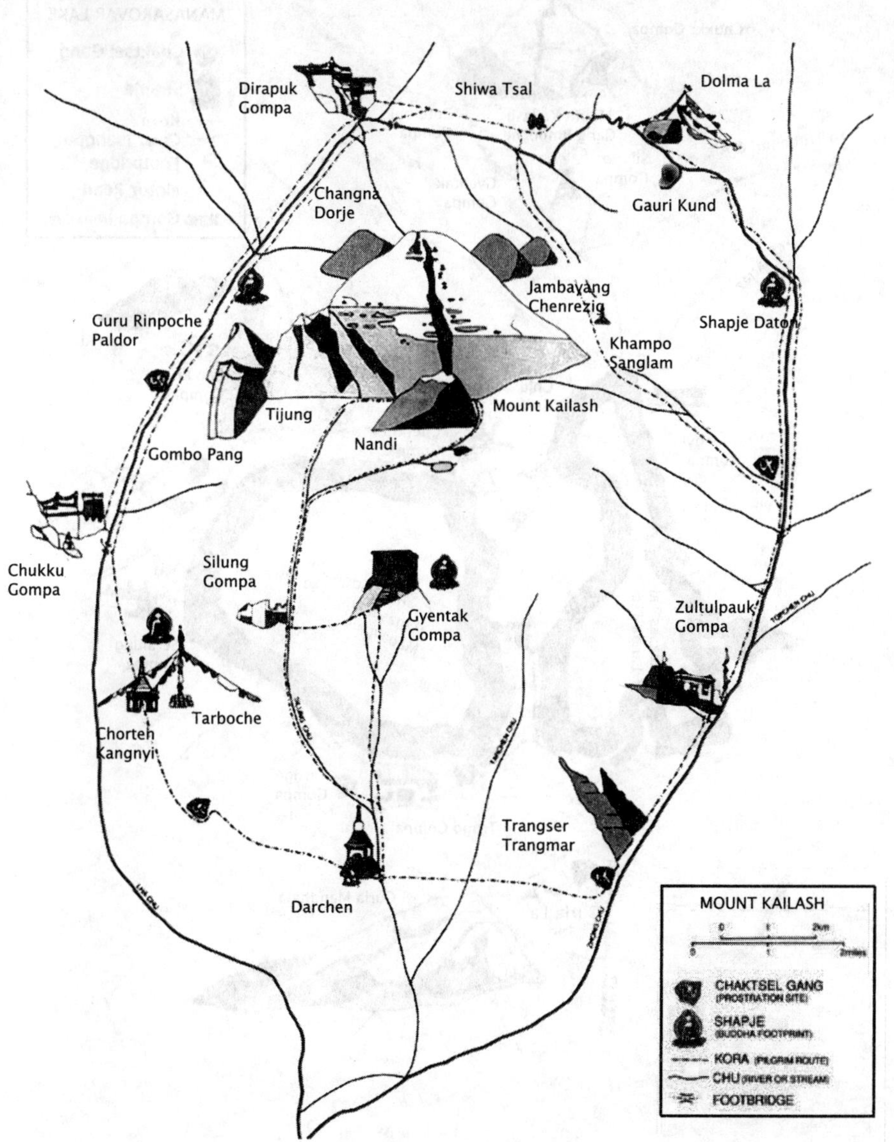

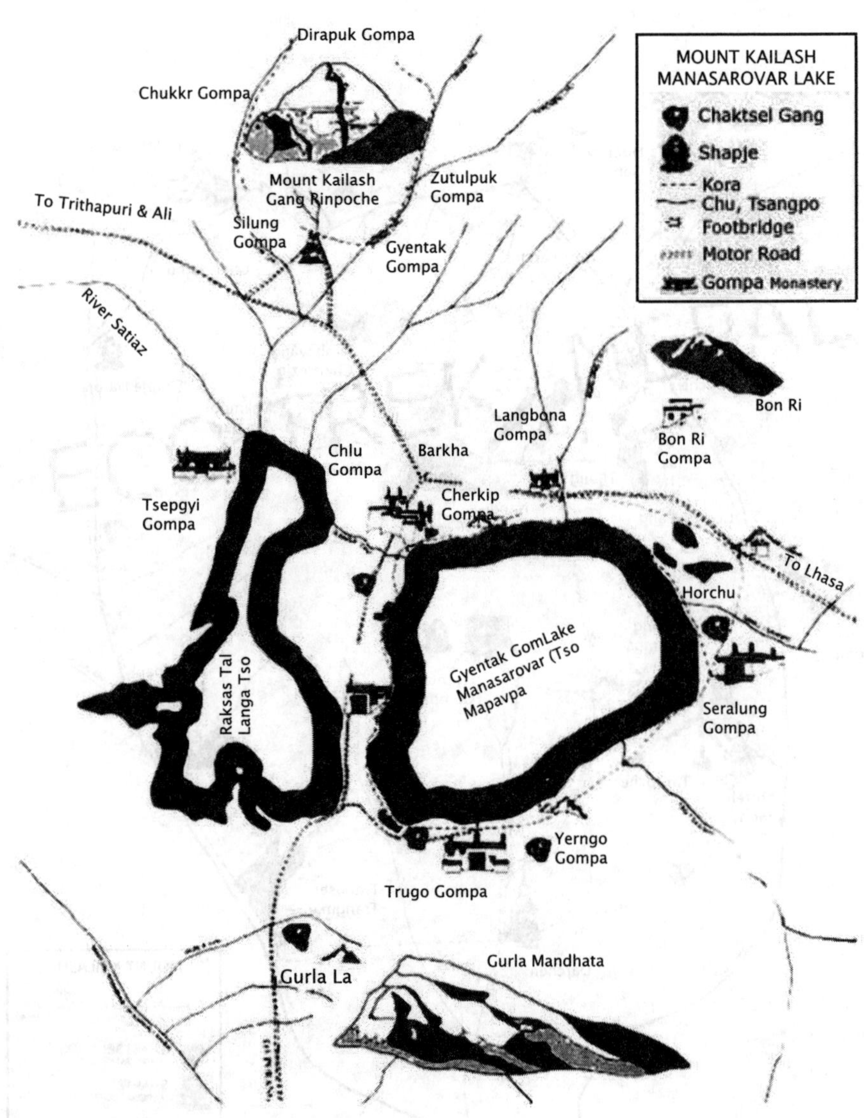

MOUNT KAILASH
MANASAROVAR LAKE
Chaktsel Gang
Shapje
Kora
Chu, Tsangpo
Footbridge
Motor Road
Gompa Monastery
Dirapuk Gompa
Chukkr Gompa
Mount Kailash
Gang Rinpoche
Zutulpuk
Gompa
To Trithapuri & Ali
Silung
Gompa
Gyentak
Gompa
River Satiaz
Bon Ri
Langbona
Gompa
Bon Ri
Gompa
Chlu
Gompa
Barkha
Tsepgyi
Gompa
Cherkip
Gomna
To Lhasa
Horchu
Raksas Tal
Langa Tso
Gyentak GomLake
Manasarovar (Tso
Mapavpa
Seralung
Gompa
Yerngo
Gompa
Trugo Gompa
Gurla La
Gurla Mandhata